HAND-BOOK OF

SCREEN PRINTING

WITH PROCESSES & TECHNOLOGY

HAND-BOOK OF
SCREEN PRINTING
WITH PROCESSES & TECHNOLOGY

Written By
EIRI Board Of Consultants & Engineers

ENGINEERS INDIA RESEARCH INSTITUTE
4449, Nai Sarak, Main Road, Delhi - 110 006 (INDIA)
Ph. : 91-11-23918117, 23916431, 23840361, 31082370
Fax : 91-11-2391 6431, 2391 8117
* E–Mail : eirisidi@bol.net.in, eiri@eiriindia.org
* Website : www.eiriindia.org

Sole Distributor :
India Institute Of Consultants, 4/27 Roop Nagar, Delhi-07

Printed & Published By

ENGINEERS INDIA RESEARCH INSTITUTE

4449, Nai Sarak, Main Road, Delhi - 110 006 (INDIA)
Ph. : 91-11-23918117, 23916431, 23840361, 31082370
Fax : 91-11-2391 6431, 2391 8117
* E–Mail : eirisidi@bol.net.in, eiri@eiriindia.org
* Website : www.eiriindia.org

Distributed By

Small Industry Research Institute (SIRI)
Indian Institute Of Consultants (IIC)

ISBN : 81-86732-63-2
Printed in New Delhi (INDIA)

Rs. 350

Printed & Published by Sudhir Gupta for "Engineers India Research Institute"
4449, Nai Sarak, Main Road, New Delhi-110 006

Preface

The book **Hand-Book of Screen Printing with Processes & Technology** covers almost all the basic and advanced details to setup own Screen Printing Unit. The new edition of the book is covering latest methods including Screen Printing, Screen Printing on Paper, Textiles and Other Printing Substrates, Screen-Process Stencils, Screen Printing Automatic Press, Choosing A Printing Process, Screen Printing Inks, Screen Printing Accessories, Stencils, Chemicals Used and Formulations, Common Faults in Screen Printing, Printing Unit, Automatic Screen Printing Machine, Screen Printing on Different Surfaces, Inks For Screen Printing, Adhesives, Screen Printing on Glass, Colour Combination, Silk Screen Photo Stencil Preparation, Plant Economics of Screen Printing on Cotton, Polyester & Acrylic, Plant Economics of Heat Transfer Label By Screen Printing Process, Plant Economics of Cloth Printing, Plant Economics of Screen Printing, Plant Economics of Screen Printing Inks, Plant Economics of Screen Printing on Paper/Cards, Plant Economics of Screen Printing on Cotton Cloth, Suppliers of Machinery, Suppliers of Raw Materials, Details of Screen Printing Machinery.

The book has been written for the benefit and to prove an asset and a handy reference guide in the hands of new entrepreneurs and well established industrialists.

Director

ENGINEERS INDIA RESEARCH INSTITUTE

4449, Nai Sarak, Main Road, Delhi - 110 006 (INDIA)

E–Mail : eirisidi@bol.net.in, eiri@eiriindia.org

CONTENTS

1

Screen Printing

Screen-process printing can be accomplished with only a minimum amount of equipment. Basically all that is required is a press, a squeegee, and a place to dry your prints. While you can buy a hand-operated screen-printing press for relatively little money, even house wives can also easily make one.

The Screen-Printing Press

A hand-operated screen printing press. The basic parts of (as shown in the Figure A) are the frame, base, screen fabric, and squeegee.

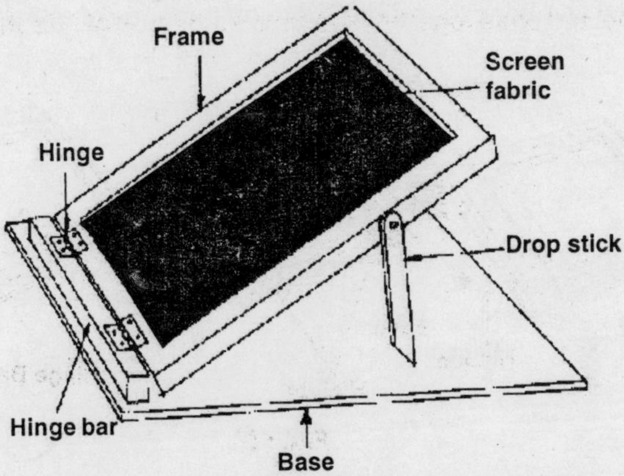

Fig. : A

The *Frame* serves as a support for the screen fabric. It can be made from wood, metal, or any other rigid material. However, a soft, straight grained wood such as pine or popular is generally utilized for this purpose. Miter, end lap, or spline joints may be used to fasten the corners of the frame together. Each of these joints are illustrated in Fig. B. Angle and corner irons are sometimes used to reinforce the corners of a large screen-printing frame, Fig. C

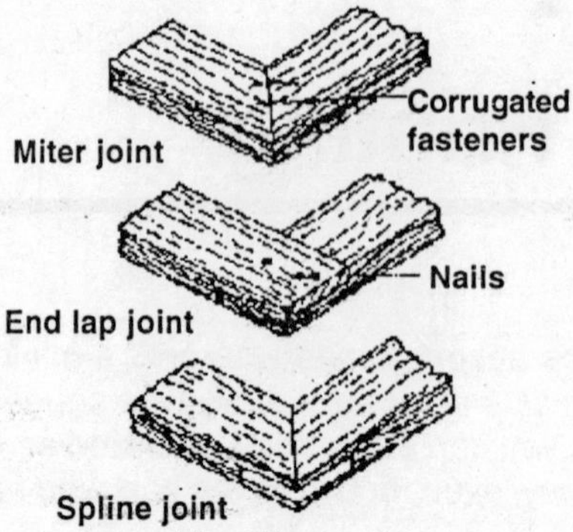

Fig. : B

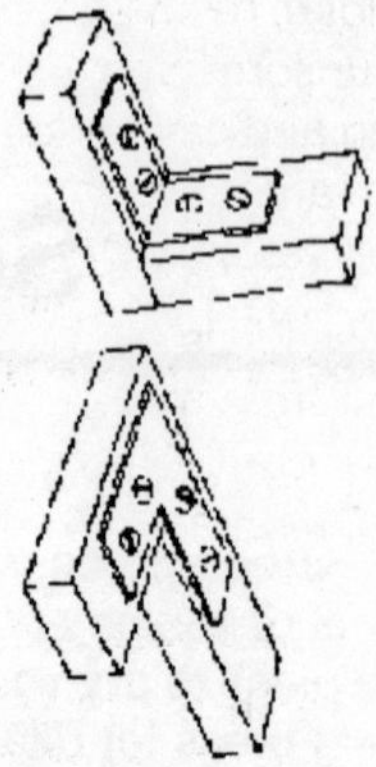

Fig. : C

The base of the press is the surface upon which the substrate (material to be printed upon) is positioned and held during printing. It is usually made from a thin sheet of plywood or hardboard that has been cut slightly larger than the outside dimensions of the frame. Loose-pin butt hinges serve to hold the frame and base together. Common methods of attaching the frame to its

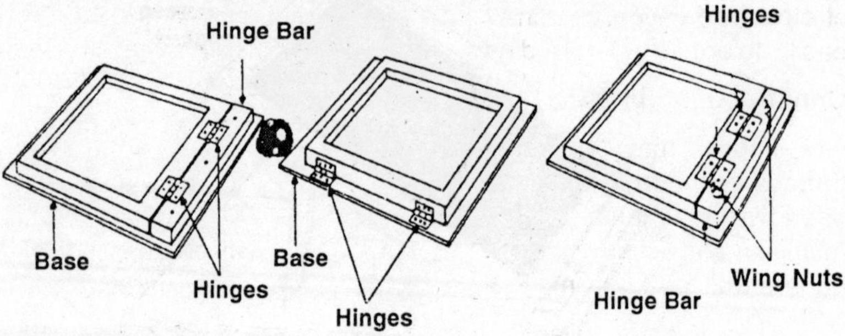

Fig. : D

The *screen fabric* is a piece of woven material, that is stretched tightly across the frame. It serves to carry the stencil throughout the printing run. Three important factors must be considered when selecting a fabric for your screen-printing press. These include the type of material from which the fabric is made, how the fabric is constructed, and the size and number of openings in the screen fabric through which ink can pass.

Types of Fabrics

Silk, polyester, nylon, and metal wire are the materials, that are most often used to make screen fabrics. Silk is a natural fiber produced by the silkworm as it spins its cocoon. Polyesters such as Dacron. Terial, and Polylast are synthetics. They are man-made from materials containing cellulose, resins,and hydrocarbons. Polyester fabrics are characterized by their uniform weave and good dimensional stabilty. They are also extremely strong and can be used for long runs even on abrasive substrates. A major disadvantage is that indirect photographic stencils will not adhere as well to polyesters as they will to silks.

Nylon is also a synthetic. Like polyesters, nylon fabrics are uniformly woven from man-made fabrics that are both strong and durable. Because of their durability, nylon fabrics can be used for long runs on rough and, or, uneven surfaces. Because of their uniformity of weave, nylon fabrics are capable of laying down an even layer of ink on these surfaces. Unlike polyesters, however, nylon fabrics lack dimensional stability. They tend to stretchwith use. Nylon fabrics will also absorb moisture and react to temperature and humidity changes. To maintain print registration and screen life, nylon fabrics must be very taut on the screen-printing frame. It is a good idea to first wet a nylon fabric before stretching it on the printing frame.

Fabrics woven from copper or stainless steel wires are available for printing long-run commercial work while maintaining accurate registration throughout the run. Metal fabrics are expensive. They are also difficult to stretch. Use caution when working with metal fabrics. These fabrics are easily deformed or kinuked as a result of too much pressure or mishanding.

Construction of Fabrics

Fabrics may be woven from either multifilament or monofilament threads. Multifilament threads are made from very fine fibers that have been twisted together. Both silk and poleyster type fabrics are offered in multifilament construction. Hand-cut and indirect photographic stencils adhere well to fabrics made from coarse, multifilament threads.

Monofilament threads are made from single strands of manmade fibers or from metal wires. Nylon, stainless steel, copper, and some of polyester fabrics are of monofilament construction. To obtain good stencil adhesion on this type of fabric, it is generally necessary to roughen the surface of the threads. Various types of abrasives are available for this purpose.

Mesh Count, Mesh Strength, and Mesh Opening.

The coarsness or fineness of a screen fabric depends upon its *mesh count* or the number of threads per inch of fabric. Multifilament fabrics such as silk and some polyesters may have as few as twenty to as many as 200 threads per inch. Monofilament fabrics may have upward of 400 threads per inch. The mesh count for multifilament fabrics is generally indicated by a number ranging from 1 to 25. The higher the number, the greater the mesh count and the finer the fabric weave.

Number 12 silk or its equivalent can be used for most general purpose screen- process work. A number 14 or finer screen should be employed when printing detailed line illustrations. For coarse work, a number 8 or10 mesh screen will suffice. Monofilament fabrics should be used when reproducing halftones by the screen process. The mesh count needed will depend upon the halftone screen ruling that was used to prepare the required film positive. Fabric with a mesh count that is at least 3-1/2 to four times that of the halftone screen ruling is recommended.

STRETCHING THE SCREEN FABRIC

Stretching involves tensioning and attaching the screen fabric to the printing frame. The optimum tension that is required will vary with the type of fabric used. An airoperated fabric tensioning device is designed to stretch all types of screen fabrics, including stainless steel mesh. While such a device is helpful, it is not required for most work. Drum-tight screens can also be stretched by hand.

The screen fabric may be attatched to the frame, with staples or by inserting heavy cord into grooves that have been cut into each side of the frame. If staples are utilized, attach the fabric as shown in Fig. E. Use a heavy-duty staple gun to first staple the center of each side of the fabric to the center of each side of the frame. Then, while pulling a corner of the fabric taut with one hand, begin to staple along one long side of the frame. Work from the center, outward. Locate a staple approximately every half inch until you reach the corner of the frame. Now go back to the center of the same side of the frame and repeat the procedure. Then staple the other long side from center to ends. Finally, repeat the procedure along the short sides of the frame.

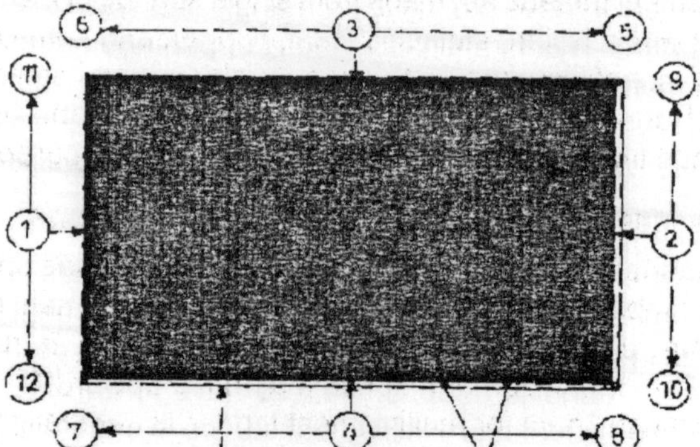

Fig. : E

To attach the fabric with cord one must cut a groove down the center of each side of the frame. Cutting may be done with a table saw, or frame stock may be purchased with the groove already cut. The relationship between the diameter (thickness) of the cord and the depth and width of the groove that is required, is illustrated in Fig. F. Stretching is accomplished by first covering the groove side of the frame, with a piece of screen fabric that has been cut to the outside dimensions of the frame. Then a dull-edged tool is used to press a continuous length of cord down into the grooves. It is advisable not to press the cord down completely the first time around. Instead circle the frame with tool two even three times, each time press somewhat harder on the cord. This will help to ensure a more uniform tension on the screen fabric.

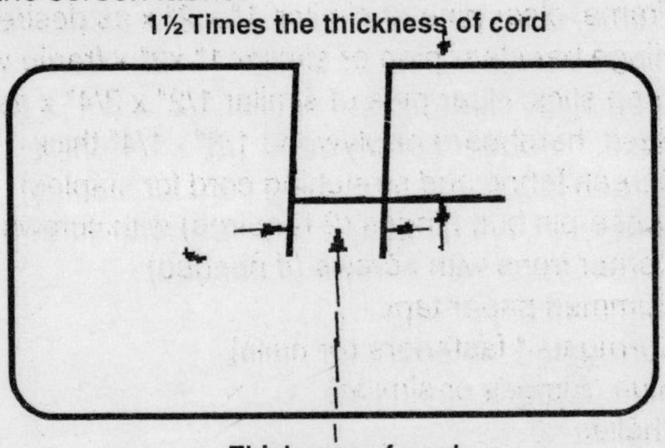

Fig. : F

The *squeegee* is used to spread ink across the screen and to force it through the stencil onto the substrate below. It consists of a hard rubber blade held in a wooden handle, Fig. G. The blade is generally between 3/16 and 1/2 inch thick. Blades shape will depend upon the requirements of the job to be printed.

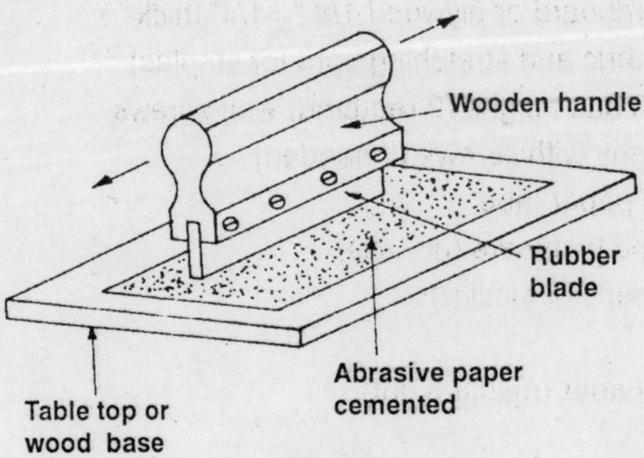

Fig. : G

How to Build A Screen-Process Press ?

Instruction for building the screen-process press. These dimensions, of course, will depend upon the sizes of the jobs to be printed. (Suggested inside frame dimensions for a general purpose screen process press are 14" x 21").

Step 1 : Assemble Needed Materials

Gather the materials as specified in Fig H

BILL OF MATERIALS
Frame, clear pine of similar. 1" x 2" x as desired
Hinge bar clear pine or similar 1" x2" x frame width
Drop stick, clear pine of similar 1/2" x 3/4" x as needed
Base, hardboard or plywood 1/8" - 1/4" thick
Screen fabric and stretching cord for staples)
Loose-pin butt hinges (2 required) with screws
Corner irons with screws (if needed)
Gummed paper tape
Corrugated fasteners (or nails)
Glue (Elmer's or similar)
Shellac
Abrasive paper (medium grit)

Fig. : H

Bill of Materials

Frame, clear pine of similar 1" x 2" x as desired
Hinger bar clear pine or similar 1" x 2" x frame width
Drop stick, clear pine of similar 1/2 x 3/4" x as needed
Base, hardboard or plywood 1/8 " - 1/4" thick
Screen fabric and stretching cord for staples)
Loose-pin butt hinges (2 required) with screws
Corner irons with screws (if needed)
Gummed paper tape
Corrugated fasteners (or nails)
Glue (Elmer's or similar)
Shellac
Abrasive paper (medium grit)

Step 2 : Construct the Frame

Constructing a grooved frame with mitered corners can be used to fasten frame corners together.

Cut a groove down the center of the frame stock with a table saw.

Now cut the frame stock into the strips that are required to form the frame .Two long strips and two short strips are needed. Use a miter box to cut the ends of each strip at a 45-degree angle.

Glue one long strip to one short strip, as pictured in Fig. 1, then reinforce the joint with nails or with a corrugated fastener. Repeat this procedure until all four sides of the frame are joined. Now that angle irons can be used to rein force the corners of large frames complete the frame by smoothing and removing all sharp edges from the wood with a piece of abrasive paper.

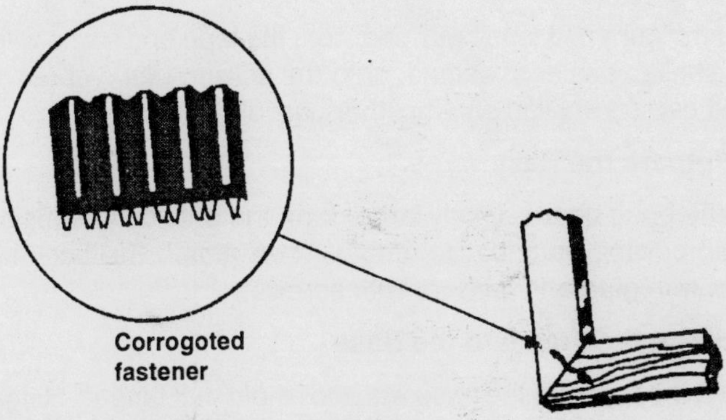

Fig. : I

Step 3 : Attach the Screen Fabric

Cut the screen fabric to the outside dimensions of the frame. Then stretch and attach it. Be sure the fabric is tight on the frame before proceeding.

Step 4 : Tape and Seal the Screen

Taping and sealing serves to extend the life of the screen. It also simplifies cleanup after a press run. Taping is accomplished by applying gummed paper tape to both sides of the screen , as illustrated in Fig. J. Wet the gummed side of the tape with a glue- water mixture before applying. The tape should extend onto the screen approximately 1/2 inch.

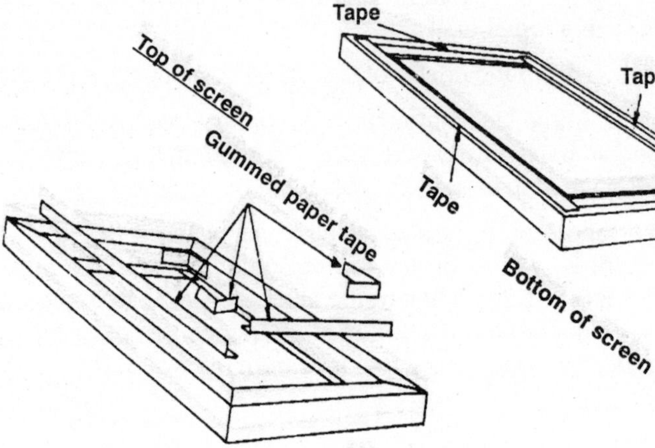

Fig. : J

After the gummed tape has dried, coat the tape and frame with shellac. Allow the shellac sealer to extend onto the screen fabric about 1/8 to 1/4 inch. Avoid getting shellac on any other part of the fabric.

Step 5 : Prepare the Base

Cut the base board slightly larger than the outside dimensions of the frame. Also cut the back bar to length. Then attach the back bar to the baseboard with glue and nails, or with screws.

Step 6 : Hinge the Frame to the Base

Attach the frame to the base with loose-pin butt hinges. Hinge clamps are sometimes substituted for loose-pin butt hinges. Such clamps may be attached to the baseboard or fastened directly to a table. When fastened to a table, the table top serves as the base of the screen-process press.

Step 7 : Add a Frame Support

A Frame support is used to keep the screen away from the base, while loading and unloading the printing stock. Three methods of providing this support are illustrated in Fig. K. The use of a drop stick represents the simplest technique. Counterweighted and spring-loaded supports, however will lift the frame, automatically, after each print is made.

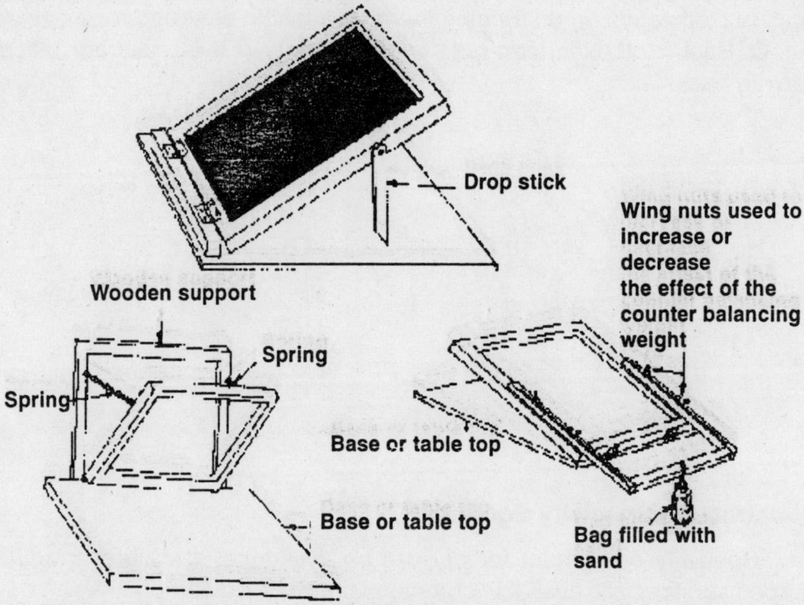

Fig. : K

Print Dry Equipment

Wet prints may be conveniently dried on either a homemade rack or on a line. An easy to build *drying rack* is shown in fig. L. It consists of individual shelves made from corrugated cardboard and narrow strips of wood. Two strips are nailed together along each end of the cardboard. Fig. M. To use, simple pile the shelves, one upon another, as each is filled with wet prints.

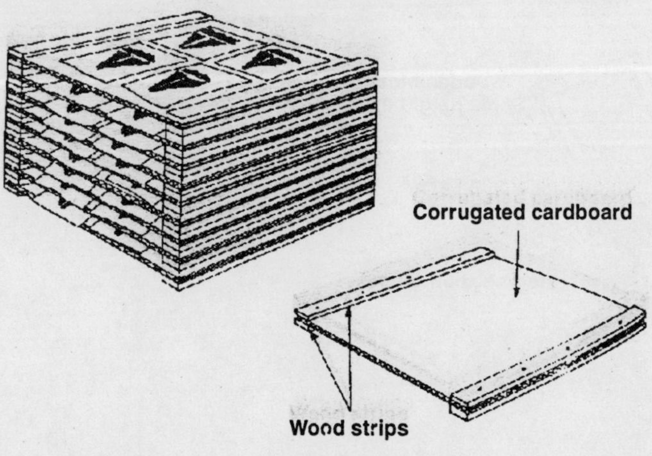

A *drying line* is pictured in Fig. N. It is made by drilling holes in the flat ends of clothespins and stringing them on a length of strong rope or wire, Fig. O. Each clothespin can hold two wet prints, if the prints are placed back to back.

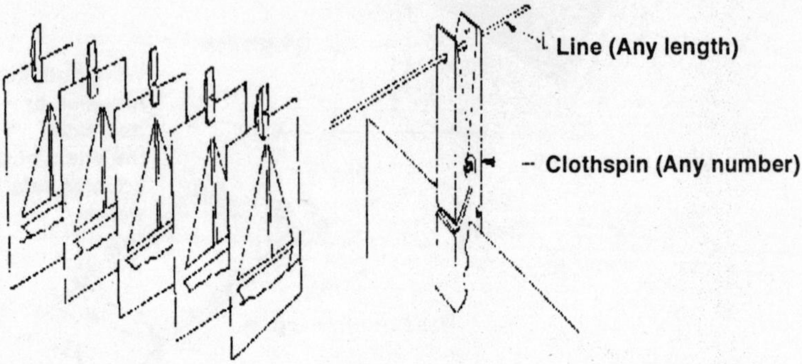

Constructing Specialty Equipment

Specialty equipment for printing on cylindrical and other irregular shaped surfaces are available commercially. Such equipment may also be constructed by the screen process printer. A homemade apparatus for printing on boxes and other thick objects is picture in Fig. P.

The operating principle of a press designed for printing on cylindrical objects is presented in Fig. Q. Note how the squeegee is held stationary, while the screen is able to move back and forth. Note also how the round object will rotate because of the movement of the screen during the printing operations.

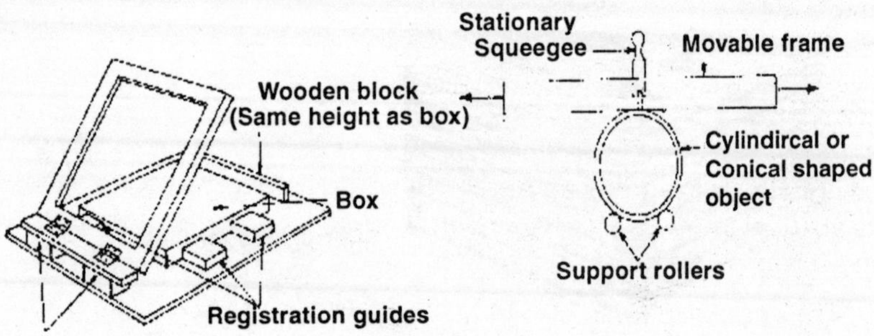

General plans for constructing a screen-process press than can be used to print on cylindrical objects are provided in Fig. R. It consists of five major parts. These include the housing, carrier, carriage, screen and squeegee.

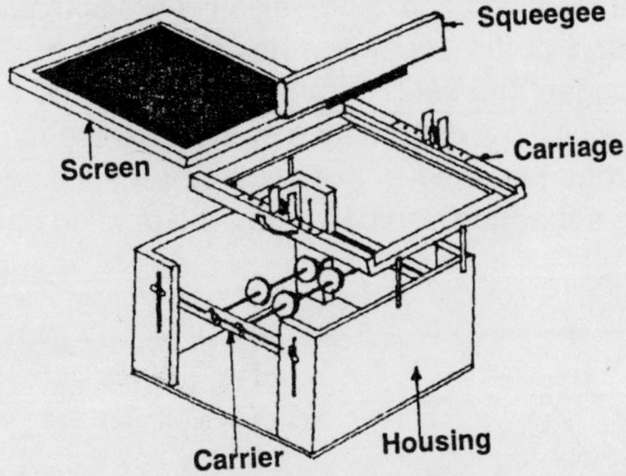

The *housing* may be made from solid lumber, plywood, or particle board. Three - quarter-inch thick material is suggested. Fasten the parts of the housing together with glue and a nails or screws. Once completed, the housing will be used to position and hold the carrier.

The *carrier* may be from threaded steel or brass rods, that measure at least 1-4 inch in diameter. Two rods are required. At least two wheels are placed on each rod. The wheels may be made from wood (for example, from a Tinkertov set). Metal (for example, from an Erector set), rubber (for example, wheels from a toy car), or some other material. The wheels must be able to turn freely on the rods. Roller skate wheel are ideal in this regard. The end of the rods are festened with wing nuts to slotted strips of metal that are positioned across the two open sides of the housing. Note that each of the two strips of slotted metal can be moved vertically within the housing. This makes it possible to print on different diameter cylinders. Note also that the slotted strips move independently of one another. Because of this it is possible to print on tapered as well as cylindrical surfaces.

The *carriage* may be hinged to the housing with strips of band iron as shown. Hinging the carriage in this manner allows for the easy insertion and removal of cylinders. The carriage may also be fastened to the housing with regular hinges. Construct the carriage from solid lumber. It is a good idea to reinforce the corners of the carriage with corner irons. Position the corner irons so that will not interfere with the movement of the screen.

The *screen* is free to slide within the track formed by the sides of the carriage. Procedures for constructing the screen are the same as those given previously.

Finally, the *squeegee* is constructed and positioned over the screen, Fig S. Note that blade is narrower than the inside dimension of the frame and that it has a beveled edge. Note, also the holes that have been drilled through either end of the squeegee handle. These holes are needed to position the sqeegee and keep it from moving with the screen. Screws or dowels located along opposite edges of the carriage must fit these holes exactly. Angle irons fastened to the carriage on either side of the handle help to keep the squeegee vertical during the printing operation.

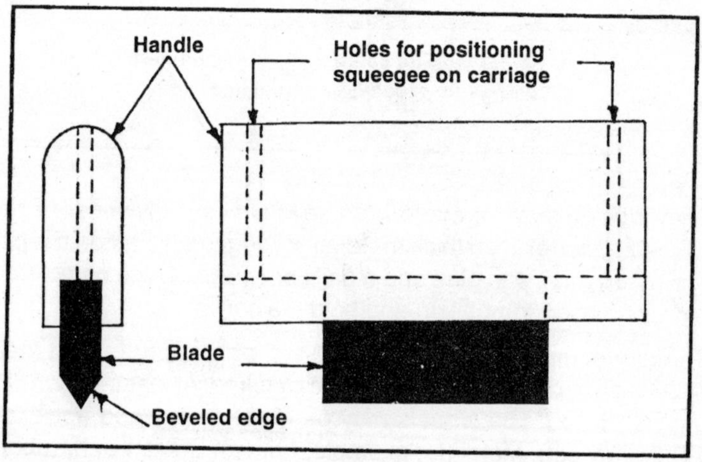

Fig. : S

2

Screen Printing on Paper, Textiles and Other Printing Substrates

A *substrate* is the base material upon which printing is done. The substrate receives and holds the screen- process printed image.

A wide variety of materials can be used as substrates in the screen process. By far the most important of these materials are papers and textiles, other common substrate categories include plastics, metals, woods, and ceramics.

Type of Paper

The screen process can be used to print on all papers and paperboards (cardboards), including those that offer a problem to letterpress, gravure, and lithography. Papers that are commonly printed by the screen process are listed in Fig. 2.1.

Textiles

No one knows exactly when textiles were invented or by whom. However, archeological evidence suggests that out ancestors were producing and using textiles many thousands of years ago. Indeed, strands of linen fish nets have been found in Swiss lake dwellings thought to be at least 10,000 years old.

Originally the term textiles only applied to woven fabrics. Today, however, it generally includes any type of cloth made from fibers, whether woven, knitted, felted, or interlaced in some other way.

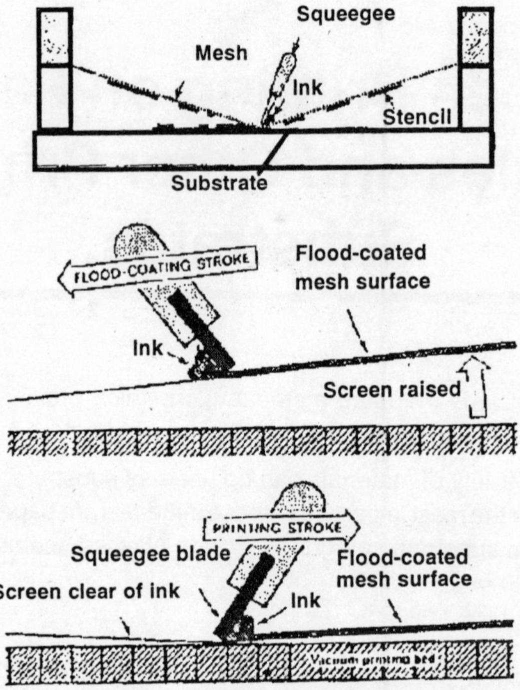

Fig. : 2.1

PRINCIPLE OF SCREEN PROCESS PRINTING
COMMON TYPES OF PAPER

Type	General Uses	Basic Size (Inches)	Basic Weights (Pounds)
Bond	letterheads, direct-mail advertisements	17 x22	9, 13, 16, 20, 24
Bristol (Card)	Tickets, postcards, covers, menues, novelty items	22 ½ x 28 ½	67, 80, 100, 120, 140, 160
Bristol (Index)	Index cards, folders, records	25 ½ x 30 ½	90, 110, 140, 170
cover	covers, binders, menus, posters, tags	20 x 26	Coated : 60, 65, 80, 100, 125 Uncoated : 50, 65, 80, 130
Label	Labels	25 x 38	50, 60, 70
Mimeograph	Mimeograph duplicating	17 x 24	16, 20, 24
Paperboard	Advertising, displays	22 x 28	

Color of Stock

Most papers are available in a choice of colors. Indicate the precise color that is required.

Fibers constitute the basic raw materials from which textiles are made. They are first spun into yarn, then woven or interlaced in some other way to form a fabric.

Fibers may be either natural or synthetic. Natural fibers come from animals and plants. Common animal fibers include wool (from sheep and other animals) and silk (produced by the silkworm as it spins its cocoon). Cotton and flax (used to make linen) are the most important of the vegetable fibers, synthetic fibers are man-made. They are made from materials containing cellulose, resins, hydrocarbons. Nylon, polyester, rayon, acetate, and acrylic are the names of some popular synthetic fibers.

Type of Fabric

Fabrics that are commonly printed by the screen process. Uses for each type of fabric are also provided here. Fabrics made from natural fibers are the easiest to print on. They are the most ink receptive. Synthetic fabrics are more difficult to print on. Synthetic fibers are less absorbent than natural fibers. Printing on synthetics such as nylon and polyester require the use of specially formulated inks.

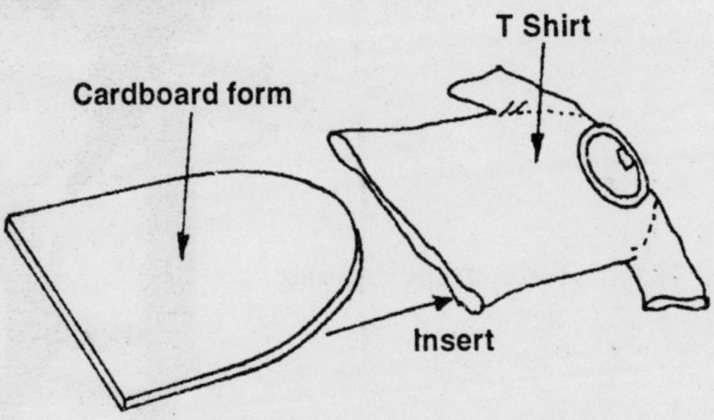

COMMON TYPE OF FABRICS

TYPE	General Uses
NATURAL	
Cotton	Napkins, T-shirts, textiles, towels
Felt	Pennants
Silk	Ribbons, textiles
SYNTHETIC	
Acetate	Drapery and upholstery
Acrylic	Added to other materials to impart crush resistance, warmth, etc.
Fiberglass	Draperies and insulating materials
Nylon	Jackets, dress fabrics, curtains
Polyester	Wash and wear apparel, curtains

Printing on T-shirts

The screen process is often used to print designs directly on T-shirts, shirts made from cotton or synthetic fibers may be imaged in this manner.

For best results the T-shirts must be free of starch or synthetic sizing. Therefore, you should prewash all sizes fabrics prior to printing. Also use a cardboard form to stretch and hold each T- shirt in position on the screen-process press, Fig. 2.2. The form, which is inserted between the front and back layers of the fabric, will prevent the inked design from bleeding through to the other side of the shirt.

Plastics

Chemists produced the first plastic material little more than 100 years ago. Since than, and particularly since World War II, many new plastics have been developed. Today, products manufactured from plastics are all around us.

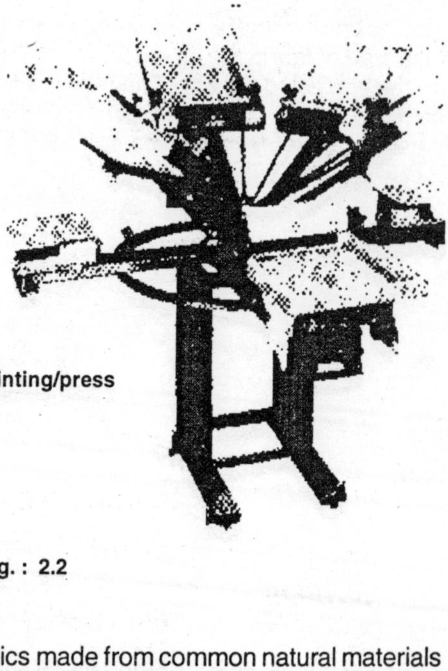

Six-colour T-shirt screen-printing/press

Fig. : 2.2

Plastics are a family of synthetics made from common natural materials such as wood, water, air, petroleum, salt, and natural gas. Heat, pressure, and chemical action serve to separate the atoms and molecules that comprise these natural materials and then recombine them to form the long molecular chains that characterize all plastics. Different types of plastics are created by slightly modifying the processes and ingredients used during manufacture.

Types of Plastics

All plastics may be classified according to their thermal properties into two groups : thermoplastics and thermosets. **Thermoplastic** materials become soft when exposed to heat and harden when cooled.Thermoplastics can be repeatedly reshaped or reformed by alternately heating then cooling the material. *Thermosetting* materials, once formed by heat and pressure, cannot be returned to their original state.

Metals

Printing on metals presents no special difficulty to the screen process. The surfaces to be printed, however, need to be completely free oxidation, corrosion, grease, and oil.

Metal traffic and street signs are often screen printed. Circuit boards that consist of metal foil laminated to a plastic base are also prepared by screening a resist on the metal surface of the board.

Woods

Woods, inculding plywoods and hardboards, are relatively easy to print upon using the screen process. Best result are obtained by first filling and, or, sealing the surface of these materials.

Fillers serve to plug the grain on open-grained woods such as oak, mahogany, and walnut. Commercial wood fillers are available for this purpose. A brush or cloth is used to first coat the wood with filler.The fillers is applied in the direction of the grain. Then, before the filler hardens, it is removed from the woods' surface. This is done with a coarse rag by wiping across the grain of the wood. The filler should be allowed to dry completely before proceeding.

Sealers are applied to woods in order to seal their surface pores. The sealer keeps the surface of the wood from being penetrated or affected by subsequent applications of printing inks. Both open-and closed-grained woods are sealed prior to printing. A mixture of one part shellac and two parts alcohol is commonly used for this purpose. The sealer should be applied with a brush. Let dry twenty-four hours before proceeding.

Solid woods are sold by the *board foot*, which is a piece of material 1 inch thick ,12 inches wide, and 12 inches long, or its equivalent. A board foot is actually a measure of volume.One board foot equals 144 cubic inches, Fig. 4.The following formulas are used to calculate board feet :

Thickness (in.) × Width (in) × Length (in.)/144= Board Feet

T" × W" × L"/144= Bd. Ft. **Or**

Thickness (in.) × Width (in) × Length (in.)/12= Board Feet

T" ×W" × L"/12= Bd. Ft.

Plywoods and hardboards (for example. Masonite) are sold by the square foot or as a standard sheet. Standard sheet size is 4 by 8 feet, or 32 square feet.

Ceramics

Ceramic materials are manufactured from earthen particles such as clay and sand (silica). Since the dawn of civilization, people have formed clay particles into useful shapes, then fused them together by baking and firing. Pottery, tiles, plumbing fixtures, dishes, and even the nose cones of some spacecraft are produced in this manner. Glass, which is one of the oldest materials, is made from melted sand. Drinking glasses, bottles, mirrors, light bulbs,and fibers for insulation and reinforcement are examples of products made from sand.

Ceramic materials are often decorated using the screen process. For example, glaze like inks can be applied to clay tiles before they are fired in the kiln, then ,when fired, these inks bond themselves to the tiles. Special inks are also available for printing on tiles after they have been fired, as well as on glass panels and mirrors. It is even possible to print on the curved surfaces of pottery and glassware using special apparatus.

3

Screen-Process Stencils

The stencil serves as the image carrier (plate) used in screen-process printing. Openings or holes in the stencil allow ink to pass through to the substrate below.The shape of the stencil openings determines the shape of the printed image. Stencils for screen-process printing may be hand cut from paper or film, painted directly on the screen, or produced photographically. Procedures for preparing each type of stencil are provided in this chapter.

Hand-Cut Paper Stencils

Paper stencils may be hand cut from just about any kind of thin paper. Kraft wrapping paper is recommended, however, because it is relatively strong and easily cut. While paper stencils are economical, they are also less durable than other types of stencils. Use them for short printing runs only. Runs greater than 100 should not be attempted with a paper stencil.

To Prepare a Paper Stencil

Step 1: Image the Paper

Cut a piece of kraft paper slightly smaller than the outside dimensions of the screen frame. Then draw the desired image directly on this piece of paper. The image may also be transferred to the kraft paper with carbon tissue.

Step 2: Cut the Stencil

Place the imaged kraft paper on a piece of smooth cardboard or a glass plate and proceed to cut the stencil. Use a sharp knife or a single edge razor blade to cut completely through the paper.

Designs may also be created by folding and cutting or tearing the kraft paper. The unfolded cut-out or the paper remaining, is then used as the stencil.

Step 3: Adhere the Stencil

Carefully transfer the cut stencil to the base of the screen-printing press. Then lower the screen almost to the base and position the stencil. After positioning , lower the screen completely and run a bead of ink across the screen with a squeegee, in Fig. :3.1. The ink acts as adhesive and will hold the stencil to the screen fabric. Finally open up the stencil image by peeling away the appropriate cut-outs from the bottom of the screen. Fig. :3.2. The stencil can now be printed.

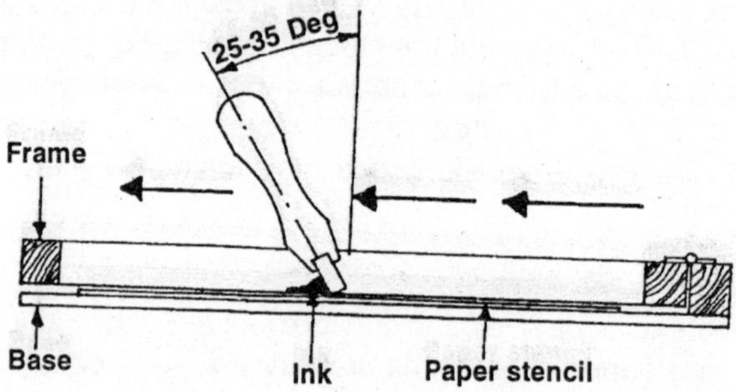

Fig. : 3.1

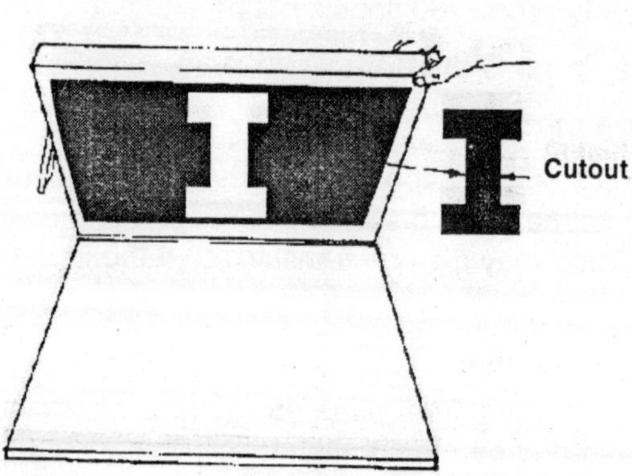

Fig. : 3.2

Hand-Cut film Stencils

Film stencils are ideal for reproducing poster size lettering and illustration, that contain many loose floating parts.They are capable of producing printed images with very sharp corners and edges.These stencils are quite durable and, unlike paper stencils, can be left on the screen after a press run. Many thousands of impressions are possible from a single hand-cut film stencil.

A cross-section of a piece of stencil film is shown in Fig.3.3. It conists of a thin layer of lacquer or water-soluble gelatin material, on a paper or plastic backing sheet. Lacquer and gelatin coated films are prepared in much the same manner.The solvents used to adhere each type of film to the screen are different, however. Lacquer films are adhered with lacquer thinner. Gelatin-coated films are adhered with water. Because lacquer films are soluble in lacquer thinner, they cannot be used with lacquer-base inks. Similarly, gelatine-coated films cannot be used with water-base inks.

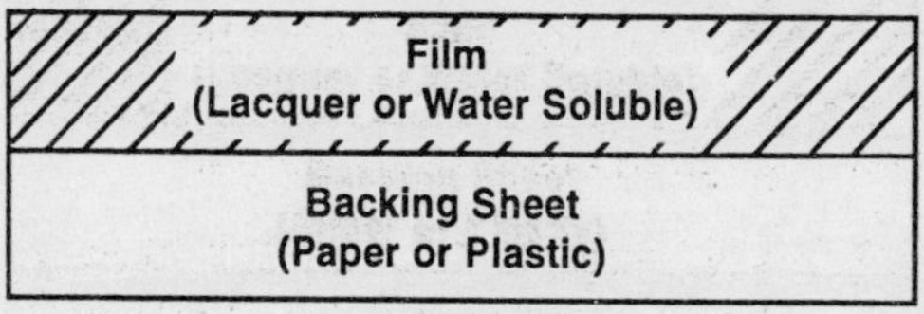

Fig. : 3.3

To Prepare a Film Stencil

Step 1 : Prepare for Cutting

Tape the design that you wish to produce to smooth, hard surface.Then cover the design with a piece of stencil film, film side up. Center the stencil film over the design and tape it in place. The design will be visible through the stencil film, the stencil can now be cut.

Step 2 : Cut the Stencil

The stencil knife is the most important. It may be used in conjunction with a metal straightedge to cut straight lines, or alone to cut curving lines thought the stencil's film layer. The stencil knife is also utilized when lifting and peeling unwanted lacquer or gelatin from the stencil. The blade in the swivel cutter is freed to revolve within its handle. This permits 360-degree manoeuverability with only the slightest touch.

Cutting must be accomplished with as little pressure as possible. The weight of the knife alone should provide sufficient cutting pressure. Do not cut into the backing sheet. The best results are obtained with an extremely sharp blade and a light, gentle touch. This excess solvent can dissolve or burn away the sharp edges of the stencil image.

Step 3 : Adhere the Stencil

Place the stencil, film side up, on a build-up board that has been cut slightly smaller than the inside dimensions of the screen-process printing frame. The build-up board should be between 1/4 and 1/2 inch thick. A sheet of glass or several layers of cardboard that have been glued together will serve nicely in this regard. Next position a clean screen over the stencil. The stencil is now ready for adhering, Fig. 3.5.

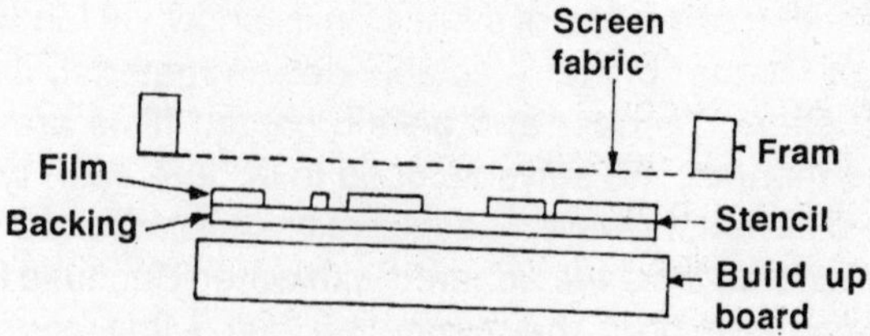

Fig. : 3.5

The overall dimensions of the stencil must be smaller than the inside dimensions of the printing screen. The stencil must not be allowed to extend onto the shellacked and taped areas of the screen.

Lacquer films are adhered to the screen with lacquer thinner. The strength of the required solution will vary with brand of film used. Gelatin films are water soluble. Some brands are adhered with plain tap water only. Other require a mixture of water and alcohol or vinegar and alcohol, as the adhering liquid.

To adhere a water-soluble stencil, saturate a sponge with the recommended solvent and move it over the fabric. Overlap your strokes until the entire surface of the stencil is wet. Aplly just enough solvent to uniformly soften the stencil film.Next blot the water-softened stencil surface Fig 3.6. Cover the screen fabric with a pad of newspaper and then roll over this pad with an ink roller. Use moderate pressure only. Repeat this procedure several times, until all of the excess water has been removed. Blotting in this manner will cause the stencil to adhere to the screen.

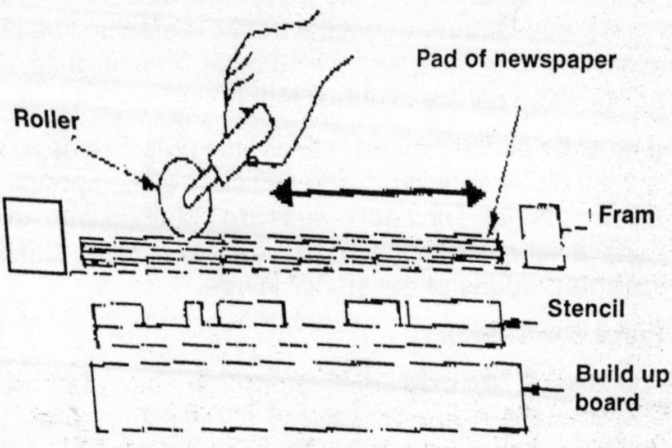

Fig. : 3.6

To adhere a lacquer stencil, dampen an absorbent cloth pad with the recommended adherent. Then, starting at one corner of the stencil, press the cloth pad against the film. The adherent will soften the film and cause it to stick to the screen fabric. Be careful not too use too much adherent or the film will begin to dissolve. Continue dampening until 4 to 6 square inches of the film's surface have been moistened. Now immediately bolt the moistened area until it is dry. Use a clean, dry rag for this purpose. Repeat the process until the entire stencil is adhered.

Too much adherent will cause the stencil film to dissolve, leaving a hole that is also a light spot.

Step 4 : Remove the Backing Sheet

Allow sufficient time for the film to dry before attempting to separate the backing sheet from the stencil. A fan or hair dryer may be used to shorten the drying time that is required. When the stencil is completely dry, use your fingernail to lift a corner of the backing sheet from the stencil. Then peel away the sheet, as shown in Fig. 3.7.

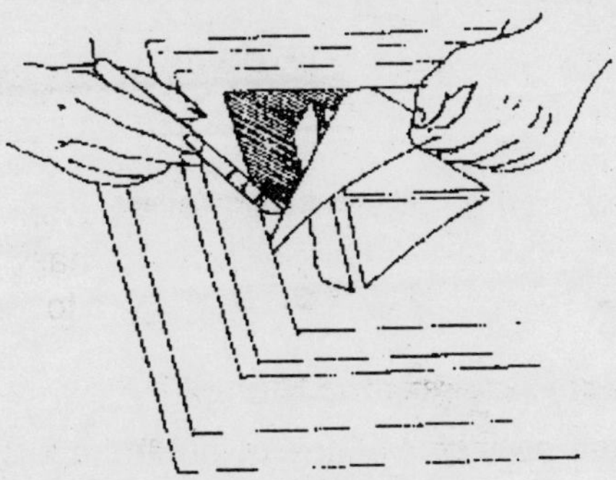

Fig. : 3.7

Photographic Stencils

Photographic stencils are used when it is necessary to reproduce fine detail by the screen process.

Positive transparencies are required to produce photographic stencils. Image areas on such transparencies must be completely opaque to actinic light. Actinic refers to the light energy that is used to harden a photographic stencil's emulsion, so that it will be insoluble in water. Non-image areas of positive transparencies may be either transparent or translucent. Non-image areas allow actinic light to pass through to the light-sensitive emulsion that forms the photographic stencil.

The positive transparency that is required can be prepared in several different ways. It may be made by drawing an India ink image directly on a piece of tracing paper or on a clean sheet of acetate. The procedures are similar to those used to prepare pictorial and technical drawing. The transparency may also be made by applying transfer type to thin plastic. Photographic processes may also be used to prepare the transparency. This is done by first preparing a line or halftone negative, then converting the negative to a positive by contact printing on process film.

There are three basic types of photographic stencils : indirect, direct, and direct/indirect.

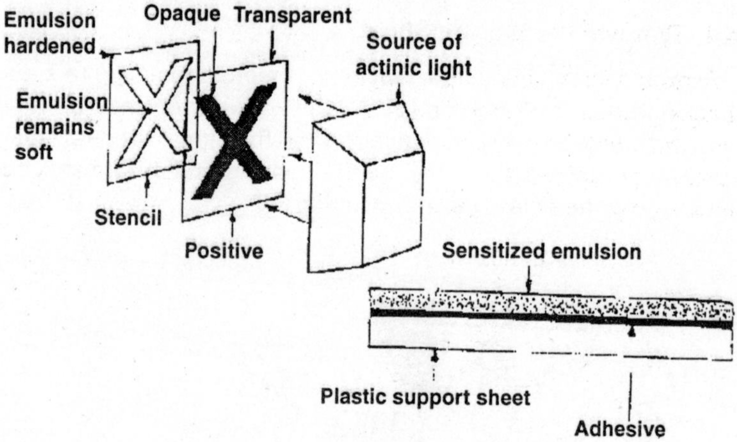

Fig. : 3.8

To Prepare an Indirect Photographic Stencil

A cross-sectional view of a piece of photographic stencil film is presented in Fig. 3.8. It consists of an emulsion layer on a plastic support sheet. The emulsion layer is sensitive to blue, violet, ultraviolet light. It is not sensitive to yellow and red light, therefore the stencil film can be handled and processed under yellow or red safelights or even under subdued incandescent illumination.

All indirect photostencil films are prepared in much the same way. They are first exposed through a positive transparency to a source of actinic light. Areas of the film that are struck by light are hardened, while unexposed areas remain soft. Processing follows exposure and serves to dissolve away the unexposed (unhardened) areas of the film's emulsion. It is these unhardened areas, that form the image during printing. After processing the film is adhered to the screen and allowed to dry. When the film is dry, the stencil's plastic support sheet is removed and the screen is ready for use.

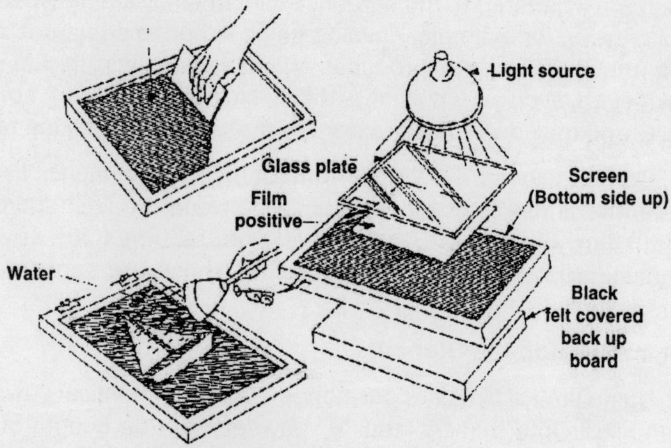

Fig. : 3.9

Step 1 : Prepare for Exposure

A vacuum-or contact-printing frame is needed to hold the positive transparency and stencil film in tight contact throughout the exposure process.

A source of actinic hight is also required. Carbon arcs emit a great amount of blue. violet, and ultraviolet radiation.

Actinic light sources emit ultraviolet light. Ultraviolet light can damage eyes. Do not look directly at the light that is used to burn (expose) a photographic stencil.

Step 2 : Load the Frame

Cut a piece of photographic stencil film so that it is at least 2 inches longer than the dimensions of the image that is to be reproduced. Place this is piece of stencil film, emulsion side down, on the rubber blanket of the vacuum frame. The emulsion side of Hi-Fi Green is its shiny side. The emulsion on most other Ulano stencil films is the duller of the two sides. Now cover the stencil film with transparent positive. The emulsion or readable side of the positive must contact the back of the stencil film.the unreadable side of the positive faces up. Next close the vacuum frame and turn on the vacuum pump. Once the air is evacuated, the positive and stencil film will be held tightly together. If a flip-top platemaker is used, turn the vacuum frame toward the light source. The stencil is now ready for exposure.

Step 3 : Expose the Stencil

Proper exposure is required if the stencil is to adhere to the screen and print correctly. Underexposure will produce an emulsion that is too thin to be readily adhered to the screen. Such an emulsion may begin to show signs of wear, for example, develop holes in non-image areas early in the press run.Overexposure produces an emulsion, that is thicker and harder than desired, such an emulsion is difficult to adhere, will not reproduce fine details, and may even crack under the pressure of the squeegee.

Correct exposure will depend upon the type of stencil film, the light source that is used, and the distance between the light source and the stencil film. Suggested starting exposure times for several films manufactured by Ulano are listed below. These are suggested starting exposure only.

Step 4 : Develop the Stencil

Ulano stencil films are developed in special chemical powders labled "A" and "B". Note that "A" and "B" powders can be bought in bulk or in premeasured foil packets.Mix 1 ounce (28 grams) of "A" and 1 1/4 ounces (35 grams) of "B" in 1 pint (0.5 liter) of water. The temperature of the water should be between 64° and 75°F (18°-24°C) Stir or shake the mixture until the powders are completely dissolved. Then pour the developer into a glass, stainless, steel, enameled, or plastic tray. The stencil can now be developed.

Quickly slide the exposed stencil film emulsion side up, into the developing tray and develop for 90 seconds. Rock the tray occasioally during the developing period. After 90 seconds the films is ready for washout.

INDIRECT PHOTOGRAPHIC STENCILS : EXPOSURE TIMES IN SECONDS*

	CARBON ARC LAMPS			***PULSED XENON***		***BLUE ACTINIC FLUORESCENT TUBES***	***No.2 Photo-Flood Bulb, 18"***
Type of film	15 amp 24" (60cm)	30 amp 24" (60cm)	40 amp 30" (75cm)	3000w 40" (110cm)	400w 40" (100cm)	built-in	
HI-FI GREEN*	336	168	198	330	250	3-5 minutes	7 ½ -8 min.
SUPER PREP*	306	153	180	330	250		" "
BLUE POLY*	272	136	160	270-300	200-225		" "
ULANO XPM*	244	122	144	270-300	200-220		" "
ULANOCRON RX*	244	122	144	300-320	225-235		" "

***Hi-Fi Green, Super Prep,Blue Poly XPM, and Ulanocron RX are registered trademarks of the Ulano Compainies.**

Step 5 : Wash Out the Stencil

When removed the stencil from the developer, the stencil image is not yet visible. Washout under running water makes the image appear. Washout temperature for several Ulano Photographic stencil films are listed here below. Set the water temperature as required before proceeding.

Place developed stencil film, emulsion side up, on a sheet of plastic or glass. The plastic or glass will serve as a support for the stencil during washout. Now place the support* on an incline in the sink basin, so that the washout water can flow over the stencil. Direct the spray across the entire surface of the film, not just the image areas. Continue washing until all of the unexposed (image) areas are dissolved from the stencil. Several minutes are usually required for complete washout.

After the image areas are completely clear, gradually lower the temperature of the washout water until it reaches the approximate temperature of the room. Chilling the stencil in this manner will harden the emulsion slightly and help to maintain image sharpness during the adhering step.

WASHOUT TEMPERATURE*

HI-Fi*	100°-115°F (44°-46°C
Super Prep*	110°-115°F (44°-46°C.
Blue Poly2-3*	97°-104°F (36°-40°C.
XPM 2*	97°-104°F(36°-40°C.
RX* 200, 300	97°-104°F(36°-40°C

Step 6 : Adhere the Stencil

The stencil must be adhered to the screen immediately after washout. Place the stencil, emulsion side up , on a hard, flat build-up board.

Adhering is accomplished by blotting the top surface of the screen with clean newsprint until the stencil' stacky emulsion meshes with the screen fabric. Do not use pressure. Simply cover the screen with newsprint and then gently wipe over the newsprint with a soft, clean rag. After blotting in this manner, change the newsprint and repeat the blotting procedure. Continue this process until color from the stencil no longer transfers to the newsprint. Normally four or five chages of newsprint are required

Allow sufficient time for the emulsion to dry before attempting to remove the stencil's plastic support sheet. A fan may be used, do not use heat, however. Heat can cause the stencil's edges to seperate from the screen. When the emulsion is completely dry, carefully peel away the plastic support sheet. The screen is now ready for printing.

To Prepare a Direct Photographic Stencil

Direct photographic stencils are prepared directly on the screen fabric. The fabric is coated with a light-sensitive emulsion; then it is exposed to a source of light through a positive transparency. Light passing through the clear areas of the positive hardens the emulsion below. Because no light passes through the opaque areas of the positive, the emulsion behind these areas remains soft, Fig 3.9. After the stencil is exposed, the unhardened ares of the emulsion are washed away with water and the stencil is ready for printing.

Direct stencil coatings are usually supplied in two parts-an emulsion and a sensitizer. The emulsion is not light sensitive until mixed with the sensitizer, which may be of the diazo or bichromate type.

Mixing, coating, exposing, and processing procedures will vary somewhat from one brand of emulsion to another. For best results, follow the instructions provided by the manufacturer of the direct emulsion coating that will be using.

Step 1 : Mix the Emulsion

The emulsion must be prepared under safelight conditions (no actinic light). Begin by dissolving the dry diazo sensitizer in lukewarm water. When completely dissolved, add the sensitizer to the emulsion and stir until a uniform color is achieved. The sensitized emulsion can now be coated on the screen or stored for future use.

Remember once sensitized, a diazo emulsion will begin to deteriorate. Refrigerated storage in a tightly caped, light tight bottle will increase the useful life of a sensitized emulsion.

Step 2 : Coat the Screen

It the emulsion has just been mixed , it should be checked for air bubbles. If none are found, coating may commence immediately. Otherwise allow the emulsion to stand until all of the air bubbles have disappeared. Air bubbles are to be avoided since they can cause an uneven coating to be applied to the screen's fabric. Also refrigerated emulsions should be allowed to return to room temperature prior to application. Emulsions thicken when they are refrigerated. Thick emulsions are difficult to apply correctly. Coating is accomplished under safelight conditions. A stiff piece of cardboard or a brush may be used, to spread the emulsion across the screen.

Step 3 : Expose the screen

Exposure requirements are similar to those described in Steps 1 through 3 of "How to Prepare an Indirect Photographic Stencil".

Step 4 : Process the Stencil

Processing is accomplished by spraying both sides of the screen with water at 600-100°F (15°-40°C). Gently spray the squeegee side of the screen, until the image areas open up,. Then intensify the spray and wash the printing side of the screen. Finally, reduce the water pressure and spray both sides of the stencil until it is completely clear and free of all foam and bubbles. The screen is now ready for printing.

To Prepare a Direct/Indirect Photographic Stencil

Direct/Indirect stencils are made from an unsensitized film that is adhered to and sensitized on the screen itself.The resulting stencil possesses both uniform thickness (characteristic of indirect stencils).

Step 1 : Sensitize the Coating Solution

The coating solution must be prepared under safelight conditions. Procedures are similar to those described in Step 1 of "How to Prepare a Direct Photographic Stencil". After the diazo powder is completely dissolved, however, it is added to a coating solution rather than to an emulsion.

Step 2 : Adhere the Film to the Fabric

Place the unsensitized stencil film, emulsion side up, on a hard, flat build-up board. The dimensions of the board should be slightly smaller than the inside dimensions of the frame. Now lower are properly roughened and decreased screen on to the stencil film.

After drying is completed (approximately 15 minutes is required when a fan is used) the plastic support sheet can be peeled from the screen.The stencil is now ready for exposure.

Step 3 : Expose the Stencil

Procedures are similar to those described in Step 3 of "How to prepere a Direct Photographic Stencil". Suggested starting exposure times for Ulano materials are listed below

Step 4 : Wash out the Stencil

Procedures are similar to those used to process a direct photographic stencils. After drying, the washed out stencil is ready for printing.

Ulano Fotocoat* Emulsion

Type	Stencil Color	Sensitizer	Description	Type of work
569	purple	diazo	unexcelled resolution : complete solvent resistance	fine details and halftones
569CL	undyed*	diazo	unexcelled resolution : complete solvent resistance	fine detailes and halftones: see -through for registration
569Fast	violet	diazo	excellent resolution : fast exposing; complete solvent resistance	fine detailes and halftones; ideal for high- volume production or weaker light sources
77112	violet	diazo	extra hardness; excellent resolution	large screens: ceramic printing: glass decorating
449	purple	diazo	complete solvent resistance wide eposure latitude	multi-purpose or special work including decals
339	undyed*	diazo	complete solvent resistance wide exposure latitude	general work: see-through for registration
TZ	light blue	diazo	water and plastisol resistant; decoratble; post-hardening unnecessary	sportswear, T-shirt and textile printing
TZ/CL	undyed*	diazo	water and plastisol resistant: decoatable ; hardening unnecessary	sportswear, T-shirt, textile printing; see-through for registration
TZ/HY-200B	undyed*	diazo	water and plastisol resistant; high viscosity	sportwear; ideal for coarse mesh; see-through for registration
FX88	blue	diazo	fast exposing; extra stencil hardness	large number of screen per day
FX88-CR	undyed*	diazo	fast exposing; complete solvent resistance	weaker light sources aggressive inks

*separate dye supplied with purchase

DIRECT PHOTOGRAPHIC EMULSIONS :
EXPOSURE TIMES IN MINUTES*

CARBON LAMPS	*ARC*	*PULSED*	*XENON*	*FLUORESCENT*	*MERCURY VAPOUR*
15 amp	40 amp	2000w	5000w	40w tubes	250w
20"	40"	20"	40"	6"	26"
(50cm)	(100cm)	(50cm)	(100cm)	(15cm)	(65cm)
1, 2/3-62/3	2,1/2-10	1-4	1 ½-6 ½	6-15	2-9

*Using screen made from white polyester fabric (305 threads per inch.)

DIRECT/INDIRECT PHOTOGRAPHIC STENCILS :
EXPOSURE TIMES IN MINUTES*

*TYPE OF DIRECT/ INDIRECT FILM ***	*CARBON LAMP*	*ARC*	*METAL*	*HALIDE*	*PULSED*	*EXNON*
	30amp	40amp	2000W	5000W	2000W	5000W
200PR	8 ½	6 ½	2 ½	1	23	5 ¾
250PR	11 ½	8 ¾	6	2 ½	30	7 ½
300PR	14	10 ¾	9 ½	3 ¾	–	9 ½
200R	15	11	4 ¼	1 ¾	23	10
250R	22	16	6 ½	2 ½	–	13
300R	30	22	8 ½	3 ¾	–	16

*Exposure time using white fabric at 40 inch distance. For distances other than 40 inches multiply times in chart by the following factors :

20 inches-0.025

30 inches-0.56

50 inches-1.56

** Registered trademarks of the Ulano Companies.

4

Screen Printing Automatic Press

The Printing Forme makes it Possible

All printing methods is essentially differ by their printing formes, however, have in common the process technological fact-apart from the screen printing method-that the printing ink is transferred from the surface of the printing forme to the substrate, either directly or indirectly: This is quite different in screen printing, for in contrast to all other printing processes in screen the printing forme is porose and this fact is decisive for all the possibilities, capabilities and the nearly unlimited fields of application of this method. This is where the decisive strong points of screen printing originate from, i.e. the versatility with all its process technological chances, the flexibility and the adaptability, the innovative strength with its innovative capacity in many industries.

The decisive factor is the screen printing forme. It consists of a frame, formerly made of wood, now in most cases either made to metal, mainly aluminium, across which the screen, either made of polyester threads or metal wires, is stretched like over a drum. The printing subject is fixed in the mesh of the screen printing fabric by barrier layers which are produced in a photomechanical way. These barrier layers, also called stencils or screen fabric in form of direct stencils or also as directed stencils be fixed at the outer side of the fabric or they can be produced as combination. The screen fabrics themselves are available in very different degrees of fineness; the standard fabric polyester 120, 120 threads per cm, is now being supplimented by essentially finer, but also many coarser fabrics. The decisive influence is that by the combination of fabrics with different degrees of fineness with possibilities of the variations in screen stencil production, i. e. by different stencil methods, the thickness if the ink layer applied can be varied and controlled. The screen printing ink is applied across the printing screen with stencils by means of squeeges, and they will get into the substrate only at the permeable spots through the mesh of the screen wire.

The Screen Printing features and their singularity

From these features of the printing forme outlined above the essential characteristics of the singularity of screen printing will result; they can best be summerized under three focal points :

The screen printing forme in the mordern version is versatile considering both its size and the form of the surface of the substrate to be printed. The means the range of possibilities for the screen printing forme goes from few sqcm up to 30 or even more sqm, and it is clear that the large sizes will remain the domain of screen printing.

The thickness of the layer in screen printing is not only thicker than in all other printing methods, but can be varied by means of the characteristics, already mentioned. In accordance with the characteristics, the durability and the effects asked for, the thickness of the layer can be altered and if necessary be extremely increased. If in normal industrial screen printing the thickness of the dry ink layer is between 5 and 7 micron, it is possible to increase the thickness of the layers in industrial processes up to 100 micron. This way the coating technological criterium of screen printing has a decisive part in many fields of application typical for screen printing across many industries. Significant examples are the production of outdoor signs with durability, but also most of the technical tasks in the industrial field. Because of these coating properties of screen printing it is not only a printing method but at the same time a qualified coating technology! Especially in this function screen printing is needed for numerous technical applications in many industrial and trade branches and for even changing and new applications.

In screen printing the making of the printing inks is not only influenced by the printing method but also by the task to be done, that is the purpose it has to serve. This way a singular versatility is reached as shown in the wide range of programmes with the many ink types and products of the screen prinitng industry.

A screen printing ink essentially needs hardly more than the fine grinding of the pigments and the press-ready adjustment. This way a most diversified range of effects is realized according to the respective requirements, e.g. highly opaque effects with high gloss, transparent effect, fluorescent effect, technical effects, and all that with a great variety of inks, so to speak the language of screen printing. The unique diversity of inks with their light intensity and their lasing properties has been advanced by new ink mixing systems and colourimetrics system; especially since the creation of the computer assisted C-Mix-Comp a variety of millions of shades for all applications can be calculated fast, precisely and economically, and realized in practice. This increased use of the variety of ink shades in screen printing shows to an even greater degree the typical close relation between ink and printing and the expressiveness of the colour by means of screen printing !

This means that on the whole the almost unlimited variety of application is the special strong point of screen printing with reference to the different materials, surfaces, purposes, and tasks.

Apart from the variety of tasks it is the extraordinary flexibility in screen printing, this flexibility for shortest, short, medium length up to long and very long runs with various sizes, combined with the effects of economic efficiency and the special surface effects that can be realized. Basically the process technology in screen printing is relatively simple and this way opens up many possibilities. Today and in future the semi-automatic technology will be needed for certain tasks and full automation has spread for many years now in form of fast running flatbed screen printing presses and cylinder screen printing presses up to the monocolour and varicoloured rotary printing technology in screen printing. The printing output has been steadily increased and at the same time the specialization in screen printing has been advanced further and further. It turned out that in the graphic screen printing sector, i.e. mainly for the production of advertising media of all kinds, especially paper posters and adhesive films/foils, a new orientation in engineering had become necessary focussing on standardization, series production, systematic further development and research, concentration and tasks to come concerning the improvement and refining of the existing technology.

The development in technical screen printing in industrial applications was quite different; in this field screen printing is not an aim of the company but an important stage in the production process. Remarkable achievements have already been realized in certain fields of production, especially in case of high-capacity screen printing presses for printing packages and labels (rotary printing) and in other special applications.

In commercial screen printing field, screen printing is the purpose of the company and the main client is the advertising industry with its wide demand for advertising media of various kinds and with different effects. This sector can be assessed to cover a market share of about 30-40% at present. In contrast the technical screen printing sector covers about 60-70% and dominates the industry with unlimited variety of different applications which are outlined above.

Apart from the variety and flexibility the third strong point of screen printing is the innovative ability which actually is a conditon for the introduction of new processes and products. The capacity for innovation shown again and again this way has been proven by significant examples in the present-day production methods both in graphic-commercial and in technical-industrical screen printing. The examples range from the production of signs to printed circuit boards, from the printing of glass to textile screen printing, from package printing to membrane keyboards in order to outline the diversity of products that are common products now and owe their existence to the innovative capacity of screen printing.

Process-technological limits have been expanded in screen printing again and again and this process will go on. Limits are expanded as regards the fineness of line and screen, the machine output, the safeguarding of printing quality and its reproducibility, the environmental orientation, the ink technology with the creation and the further development of new systems as an alternative to the highly developed conventional ink series by UV-hardening screen printing inks and water-based screen printing inks, by the continuous further development of the diversity of inks by colourimentrical systems such as C-Mix-Comp.

It is not sufficient to look at the art of printing alone and to print the jobs taken over. The ingenuity in looking for new tasks is of increasing importance for screen printing. It will become more important to realize new possibilities needed, to develop new products, to participate in new developments in the fields of substrates, inks, but also materials such as metals and plastics for industrial use, to keep up relations with producers who not only need advertising media but also have to treat the surfaces of their products and need to add marks and decorations.

On the whole that means that a good development can be expected for the future in screen printing, if it is possible to unfold the strong points even more and to realize that in the market, that means to sell the potential included in the variety of tasks, the flexibility, the innovative capacity again and again and with increasing intensity.

The graphic-commercial field of screen printing profits from the alliance with the advertising industry, which is marked by a certain degree of interdependence. Advertising is mainly depended on screen printing as regards the not extremely short-term media and their efffects, the durability, the variety and the dimensions and materials, but also as regards the flexibility when having to meet the requirements and the length of runs. The advertising industry and screen printing need each other, look for each other, depend on each other. This means that is not only important partners and clients in the advertising industry what its strong points are and to sell its effeciency effectively. The near future of screen printing will mean increasing communication tasks in the advertising industry, especially concerning the European Single Market on the one hand and the development in the East on the other hand, and the overall increase in advertising activities that is to be expected at the places where the goods are sold and probably an increasing demand for display, increasing labelling with better quality, but also more flexible fields of application in outdoor advertising, especially as regards paper poster.

The development will be quite different in technical screen printing and the development reached there in the past years with steady growth rates and increasing variety of tasks leads to the conclusion that the future has only just begun.

Within the diversified tasks in the field of electronics and production, screen printing will be needed to an increasing degree even if the economic development is not that favourable as regards the demand; the many articles and apparatuses in the field of consumer goods that will even increase in number will have to be marked, decorated, and the metallic and plastics surfaces will have to be treated. Screen printing with its suitability for printing and at the same time coating is needed to an increasing degree in those fields where large -scale production takes place. The decisive factor for the future will be, however, that the advantages of screen printing will be realized to an increasing degree and made use of.

5

Choosing A Printing Process

1. LETTER PRESS

Advantage :

Faithful Reproduction versatile & late correction or type matter even on the printing ink

Operation such as numbering & perforated can be carried out while printing..

Limitations :

Good coated paper reqd. for half tone printing inpractile for large illustrations i. e. poster, wall charts etc.

omparatively low running speed storage of type & forms expensive & space consuming.

2. LITHOGRRAPHY

Advantage :

Wide range of paper board qualities. Intricate matter can be easily handled by using art work or by stripping negatives or pos. Fast ink speed. No limitations to size of illustration (posters etc.) convenience of storage of plates or films. Letterpress books may be reprinted by photographing original. Making typesetting un-necessary.

Limitation :

Alterations to plates inpracticable.

Inferior lithography printing appear flat & dul with weak bad printing.

3. PHOTO GRAVURE

Advantage :

Rich tonal effects, in full colour mono-chrome, ideal for very long runs in colour, in expensive paper coated or un-coated (women magazine, prepress for newspaper advert etc.)

Very fast running speeds.

Limitations :

Preparatory cost expensive. Alteration to cylinder inpracticables. Cylinder storage expensive. Type matter &fine line detail becomes somewhat broken by screen pattern.

4. SCREEN PRINTING

Advantage :

Low preparatory cost suitable for short runs in multicolours, light colours & fluoroscent ink widely used.

Light colours can be printed on dark materials. Versatile use of process for printing on paper &board, fabric, plastic, wood, china pottery, glass& may be printed on curved surfaces, also used for posters, show cards, bus sides, Aeroplane body.

Limitation :

Printing speed comparatively slow. Halftone screen is limited to fairly course work.

5. COLLO TYPE

Advantage :

No screen reqd. beantiful colours, very true to two original & fairly inexpensive. Printing reels of paper, foil, plastic, film, rubber stereo long lasting.

Limitation :

Suitable for short run only (upto 1000 copies only). Printing must be colour for colour (i.e. No 4 colour process).

Only one printer commercially. Only suitable for packaging type work such as wrapping paper etc. Not suitable for type matter excepting the small quantities in large sizes.

6. FLEXO GRAPHIC

Advantages :

Fast running speed, good colour areas, suitable for printing reels of paper, foil, plastic, filn etc.

Limitation :

Only suitable for packaging type work such as wrapping paper etc. but not suitable for type matter.

What Process to use :

Making to decision each printing process involved cost in various stages. Preparatory cost are the same whether the quantity of printed matter is 15000 copies. And this must be borne in mind. Litho is the most widely used process at present because the overall cost is lower than letterpress printing & this only overtaken by Gravure when very long runs are involved. The high preparatory cost of preparing gravure cylinder is soon outweighed when a very long run is envisaged.

At the other end of the scale screen printing has low preparatory cost but the printing is either manual or semi automatic & then drying is either achieved by using racks or by passing under an infra-ray drier. Which involves a further handling charge, cosequently long run becomes costly.

6

Screen Printing Inks

Inks for screen printing are available in a rainbow of colors. Each type of screen printing ink has a binder suited to a specific class of substrate. Screen inks are formulated to be short and buttery for sharp squeegee transfer. These ink solvent should not evaporate rapidly. Rapid solvent evaporation would cause screen clogging during the printing process. Table 6.1 lists the many types of ink and substrates available to the screen printer.

Table 6.1. Screen printing inks and substrates

Ink Types	*Substrates*
Water soluble	Paper
Lacquer	Cardboard
Plastics	Textiles
Enamels	Wood
Metallic	Metals and foil
Ceramic	Glass
Electrical conducting	Lacquer-coated fabrics
Etching	Masonite
Luminescent	All plastics
Fluorescent	

Poster Ink

Inks whose end use is to produce point-of-purchase (PoP) displays, posters, wallpaper, outdoor billboards, greeting cards, and packaging materials are classified as poster inks. The following list identifies major poster inks and their uses:

Flat poster ink : Recommended for printing on paper and board stocks. Dries by solvent evaporation in about 20 minutes or can be force dried with special driers in seconds. Produces a flat finish and is used for displays, posters, and wallpaper.

Satin poster ink and halftone colors : Recommended for printing on paper and cardboard displays. Dries by solvent evaporation in about 20 to 30 minutes or can be force dried in seconds. Are used to print PoP displays, posters, outdoor billboards, greeting cards, and packaging materials. Standard colors are opaque; halftone colors are transparent.

Gloss poster inks : Produce a hard gloss finish and are formulated for paper and board stocks. Are used to print PoP displays, posters, greeting cards, corrugated displays, and packaging materials. Dry by evaporation in about 15 to 20 minutes or can be force dried in seconds.

Economy poster inks : Much like flat poster ink series but lack the outdoor durability of flat poster ink.Made for supermarket and chain store applications. Dry to a flat finish in about 20 to 30 minutes by evaporation or can be force dried in seconds.

24-Sheet poster ink : Formulated mainly for outdoor use. Are waterproof and flexible and can withstand finishing processes such as die cutting, creasing and folding. Recommended for posters, outdoor displays, sign cloth, and bumber stickers. Dry by evaporation in about 20 to 30 minutes or can be force dried.

Enamel Ink

Enamels are inks that flow to a smooth coat and usually dry to a glossy appearance slowly. Because enamels penetrate the substrate less than do poster inks and dry mainly by oxidation, their drying times are much longer. Enamel inks include gloss enamel (normal and fast dry), synthetic gloss enamel, and halftone enamel.

Gloss Enamel

Gloss enamels are used to image substrates such as wood, metal, glass, paper, cardboard, and fiber drums. They are also used as an adhesive base for flocking or beads in a variety of decorative products. Normal gloss enamels dry by oxidation and should be allowed to stand overnight. In addition to the substrates listed for gloss enamel, fast-dry gloss enamels are commonly used to image polyethylene bottles and lacquer-coated fabrics. This formulation will air dry in approximately 60 minutes or it can be cured (dry and usable) in about five minutes at 180°F (82°C)

Synthetic Gloss Enamels

Synthetic gloss enamels have high durability and are excellent outdoor inks. The synthetic vehicle adhere to a wide variety of surfaces. These enamels are great for imaging metal, wood, masonite, glass, anodized aluminium, some types of plastics, novelty toys, synthetic decals, and packaging containers. They dry by oxidation in 4 to 6 hours or can be cured at 180°F (82°C) in about 30 minutes.

Halftone Enamels

Halftone enamels are formulated to give the special hues required for halftone process work. They are made to be durable under outdoor conditions. Halftone enamels are used on the same substrates as synthetic gloss enamels. Halftone vehicles dry to a satin finish (instead of a gloss finish) in 4 to 6 hours or can be cured in 30 minutes at 180°F (82°C). All halftone enamels are transparent inks.

Lacquer Ink

There are basically two types of lacquer inks:

A general industrial lacquer ink that can produce a gloss or flat, hard finish with excellent adhesion to a wide variety of finishes.

A lacquer ink specifically formulated for making decals or printing on a specific substrate

Industrial Lacquer Ink

Industrial lacquer inks have numerous applications where chemical and abrasion resistance is important. They are used to image enamel, baked-urea or melamine-coated metal parts, and many polyester finishes. Because of their high opacity, lacquer inks are also popular for printing on dark colored book cover stock. In addition, they are used to image lacquer and pyroxylin surfaces, many plastics (cellulose acetate, cellulose acetate butyrate, acrylics, nitrocellulose, ethyl cellulose) and many polyesters. Wood paper, and foils can also be imaged with lacquers. Lacquer ink dries by solvent evaporation in about 30 minutes or can be jet dried in seconds. It can be cured for 10 minutes at 250°F (93°C) for industrial applications.

Decal Lacquers

Decal lacquers are made for printing decalcomanias. **Decalcomania** is the process of transferring designs from a specially printed substrate to another surface. Decalcomanias can also be printed on any surface where a flexible lacquer ink is needed. Consult the manufacturer's literature on printing procedures. Decal lacquer dries by solvent evaporation in one to two hours.

Printing on Plastic

Because so many plastic are being manufactured, a complete line of special inks is needed by screen printers. Plastic materials are either thermoplastic or thermosetting. A **thermoplastic** material is one that can be reformed. A **thermosetting** plastic cannot be reformed once it has been formed and cured.Table 6.2 lists several thermoplastic and thermosetting materials and some of their uses. Inks used to print on plastic include acrylic lacquer. vinyl, mylar, and epoxy resin inks.

Acrylic Lacquer Inks

Acrylic Lacquer inks are general purpose formulations for imaging thermoplastic substrates such as acrylics; cellulose butyrate; styrene; vinyl; and acrylontile, butadience, and styrene (ABS). They are used to image vaccum-formed products; in fact, adhesion and gloss are improved by vaccum forming.

Table 6.2 Screen printing inks, plastic substrates, and uses

Screen Printing Inks	
Print on Thermoplastic Substrates	For End Use
Acrylontile, butadiene and styrene (ABS)	Safety helmets, automotive components, refrigerator parts, and radio cases
Acrylics	Outdoor signs
Cellulose Acetate	Packaging, toys, book cover laminations, lampshades, and toothbrush handles
Cellulose Acetate butyrate	Outdoor signs and packaging materials
Polyethylene	Cosmetic packaging
Polypropylene	Housewares, medicine cups, luggage and toothpaste and bottle caps
Polystyrene	Construction, insulation, packaging, signs, displays, and refrigerator liners
Vinyl	PVC bottles, book covers, decorative tiles, and building components
Print on Thermosetting Substrates	
Melamine and Urea	Cosmetic packaging and electrical components
Phenolics	Electronics and appliance industry (excellent insulators)

Acrylic lacquer inks dry by solvent evaporation in about 30 minutes, or they can be force dried.

Vinyl Inks

Vinyl inks are naturally formulated for both rigid and flexible vinyl substrates. These include novelties, inflatables, wall coverings, and book covers. They dry by evaporation in approximately 30 minutes, or they can be force dried. The ink vehicles can be formulated to produce a flat, fluorescent, or gloss finish. Gloss vinyl inks can be vacuum formed.

Mylar Inks

Mylar inks are formulated to image untreated mylar and other polyester films. They dry by solvent evaporation in about 30 minutes, or they can be force dried.

Epoxy Resin Inks

Exposy resin inks are formulated for difficult to print surfaces such as phenolics, polyesters, melamines, silicones, and nonferrous metals and glass. Epoxy inks dry by a chemical process called polymerization and require a catalyst prior to use. Once the catalyst is added properly, the ink must stand for approximately 30 minutes. This period of time allows the catalyst to become part of the solution and to activate the polymerization process. The polymerization drying process takes approximately two or three hours and about 10 days for maximum adhesion and chemical resistance. The ink can be cured in 30 minutes at 180°F, in 10 minutes at 250°F, or in four minutes at 350°F. Epoxy inks that require no catalyst must be cured or baked and are not recommened for outdoor use. They are used on thermosetting plastic, glass, and ceramics. They dry to a flat finish and must be baked at 400°F for three minutes or at 350°F for seven minutes. This type of epoxy ink is very suitable for nomenclature printing on circuit boards that must be soldered.

Resist Inks

Resist inks include alkali removable resist, solvent removable resist, vinyl plating resist, and solder resist inks.

Alkali Removable Resist Inks

Alkali removable resist inks are ideal for print and -tech boards. They are less expensive than solvent removable resist inks (see following) and can reproduce fine lines. They cure from between 250°F to 265°F (120°C to 130°C) in about three or four minutes. Air drying takes about four or five hours. Alkali removable ink can be removed from the print-and-etch board after etching with a one to four percent solution of sodium hydroxide.

Solvent Removable Resist Ink

Only black solvent removable resist inks is formulated for plating etch-resistant operations such as circuit boards or nameplates. It has excellent adhesion and printability and resists acid such as ferric chloride, ammonium persulphate, and other common etchants. Removable etch resist ink air dries in 30 minutes or can be dried in five minutes at 200°F (93°C).

Vinyl Plating Resist Inks

Vinyl plating resist inks are also formulated for plating or etch resist operations. They air dry in approximately 30 minutes or in 10 minutes at

200°F (93°C). They can be removed after etching with trichlorethylene or xylol.

Plating Resist Inks

Plating resist inks are formulated specifically for plating operations. These inks are recommended for long plating cycles. Curing takes about 30 minutes at 200°F (93°C). The resist can be removed from the substrate with trichlorethylene or xylol.

Solder Resist Ink

Solder resist inks are alkyd melamine formulations for printing on copper or copper-treated coatings. Solder resist inks cure in 20 minutes at 250°F (140°C), in 10 minutes at 300°F (150°C) or in five minutes at 350°F (160°C).

Textile Ink

The three basic inks available to the textile printer are standard textile, plastisol, and dye inks.

Standard Textile Inks

Standard textile inks are formulated for cotton and other nonsynthetic fabrics. Ease of application makes these the most widely used inks for natural fabrics. They dry to a flat finish in about 45 minutes or can be cured in five minutes at 275°F (135°C).

Plastisol Inks

Plastisol textile inks are formulated for woven or knitted cotton and some synthetic fabrics. These inks can be printed directly onto the fabric or onto a coated release paper. When printing directly onto the fabric ,cure for three minutes at 300°F (150°C). When printing onto release paper, cure for one and a half to two minutes at 225° to 250°F (107° to 120°C). Images on release paper can be transferred to fabric with an iron or a heat transfer machine . Be sure to allow the release paper and fabric to cool before peeling away the paper backing.

Dye Inks

Dye textile inks are water-in-oil concentrated pigments that must be mixed with a clear extender. The proportions of water and oil in the mixture determine the color strength. These inks are used to image cotton, rayon, linen, some nylon, and other synthetic blends. Dye textile inks dry in three minutes at 300°F (150°C) and in five minutes at 250°F (120°C). Water-soluble stencil material cannot be used with dyes because of their water content. For best results use knife-cut lacquer or a direct emulsion when preparing the stencil.

7

Screen Printing Accessories

In the stencil or screen printing process, a stencil representing the non printing areas is applied to a silk, nylon or fine mesh screen to which the ink with little thick consistency is applied and transferred on to the substrate to be printed by scraping with a rubber squeegee.

The screen printing unit consists of a simple rectangular wooden frame with textile stretched across it. The frame with textile stretched across is attached to a based board by help of pair of hinges. Usually a spring or support is attached, to counter balance so that the screen rises automatically after each impression. The pattern or design is produced in the stencil or screen by coating those parts that should not transfer the ink with an impervious material.

Then by help of squeegee the ink is transferred onto the material to be coated. The whole system is given below.

Accessories

(a) Frame, (b) Screen, (c) Base Board, (d) Squeegee etc.

(a) Frame

The wood used to construct the frame should be well cured and straight grained. The wood should be well seasoned to avoid any dimensional changes after washing. For this, particularly hard wood is recommended as during the printing operation and after that one uses liquid generously and this may cause soft wood to warp and in turn this will pose much problem during printing. The frame must act absolutely flat on the printing base when completed.

Now-a-days many printers are using stainless steel tubes instead of wooden frames for effective printing. Stainless steel tubes have longer life and set absolutely flat on the printing base.

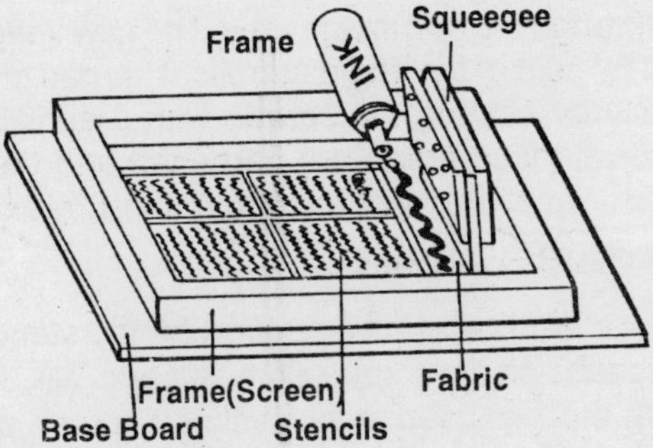

Recommended Frame Sizes : 6" x 8", 8" x 10", 10" x 12", 12" x 15", 14" x 18", 16" x 20", 18" x 24", 20" x 30", 24" x 36".

Construction of Frame

The wood should be free from knots. The size of the frame varies from 6" x 8" to 20" x 30" and the thickness of the frame varies from 2" to 4". One can take the help of professional carpenter or some one with better wood working skill. It should be kept in mind that the frame is set absolutely flat and should not 'rock' when in contact with base board. The timber should be very smooth where it will come in contact with fabrics. If not then the fabric may tear as it is stretched tight. To ensure smoothness flat file or sand paper may be used to round off all edges and corners.

(b) Screen

The screen is porous material, which allows the ink to penetrate in, by pressure of the squeegee. The image is produced by not allowing the

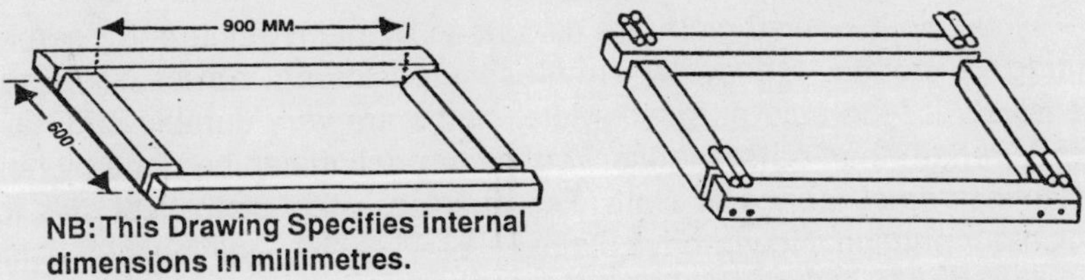

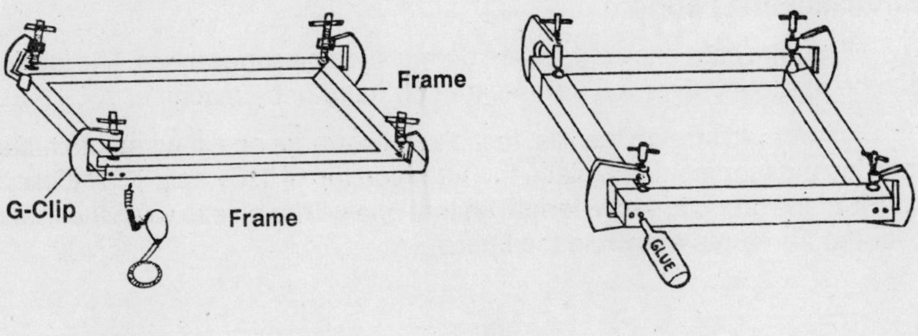

inks to penetrate through the non image area. The now image area is usually sealed or blocked by help of binding materials. This can otherwise be done photo mechanically by coating the screen with a sensitizer, exposing a positive so the non printing areas are hardened and developing out the image areas, which removes the coating from the screen in these areas.

Types of Screen Cloth or Fabrics

Screen cloth or fabric acts as a support for the stencil. The quality of printing largely depends on the screen cloth or fabric. Silk, Nylon, Organdie, Rayon, metal cloth etc. are used extensively for screen printing purpose. The screens are mainly monofilament nylon, mono and multifilament polyester, metalized polyester and stainless steel mesh fabrics.

Silk is available in the market in different sizes. The number ranges from 2XX to 25XX.

2XX to 6XX number silks have mesh size ranging from 54 to 73. 12XX to 18XX number silks have mesh size ranging from 122 to 171.

The best quality of silks which are used extensively for screen printing are 18XX to 25XX having mesh size ranging from 171 to 195.

Nylons have better durability and can be stretched tightly across the frame. Now-a-days the printers are taking advantage of nylon for it has longer durability and wide range of mesh size.

Nylon bolting cloth is available in following number (indigenous)

No. 12, 16, 20, 22, 25, 30, 35, 40 and imported such as 140 S is also available.

Metal cloth or wire cloth are also used by many printers for screen printing purposes. Generally stainless steel mesh fabrics are used extensively for the said purpose. Metal cloths are very durable and have better strength than other fabrics. Very clear printing can be done by help of stainless steel fabrics or cloth. The stainless steel cloth best suis for multicolour printing. Now-a-days stainless steel cloth is gaining increasing popularity due to its long lasting and outstanding strength.

Stretching the Fabric

Extreme care should be taken during stretching the fabrics. The fabrics can be stretched over the frame either by hand or by machine.

In order to stretch the silk, first place the frame on a flat smooth table, then lay the fabric out and place the frame on top of it. By help of a scissors cut on of the fabric an extra length so that one will be able to wrap the fabric over the frame (as shown in the figure).

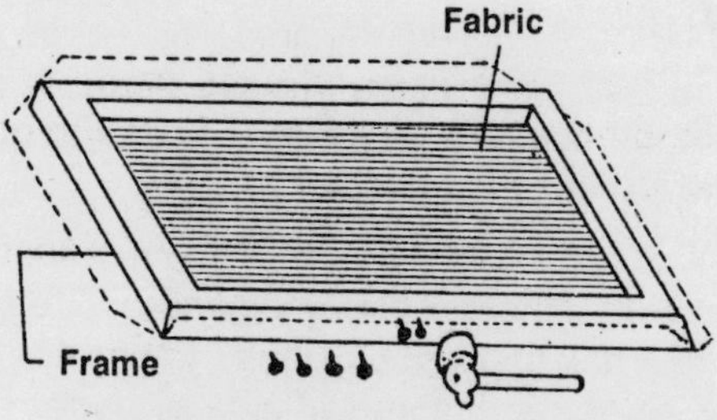

RULED PAPER HERE

To ensure correct degree of tension spread the fabric evenly along the sides of the frame and then tack it. One can remove these tacks by tactfully adjusting the tension of the screen. Otherwise it is better to insert thin bits of card board or wooden battens approximately 5mm between the frame and fabrics if one finds that desired tension is not achieved.

During stretching the fabrics it should always be kept in mind that the correct tension is achieved otherwise the printing quality will be poor.

One can find that after using the fabric several times it wears off and ink clogs appear on few places. In such case the fabric is taken off and new fabric is stretched in.

Now the screen is ready for washing. Although the cloth appears clean but usually contaminated with starch and factory grease and oils. It is very important to remove these materials otherwise the stencil will not adhere properly to the fabric. This is done by washing the screen by warm water and good grade of washing powder.

The screen is set to dry properly in a dust free area.

Blocking or Sealing

After the screen is dried properly it is advisable to coat the sides of the frame by lacquer. The lacquer coating helps in resisting the moisture, solvents and other chemicals etc. and acts as a adhesive between fabric and the frame. As soon as the lacquer dries up, a gum tape is pasted on the side of the frame, (the tack portions) are also pasted (as shown in the figure).

The gum tape is again pasted all the way around the inside of the frame so that half sticks to the frame and half to fabric. This usually prevents the ink from leaking out around the frame while printing the substrates.

Since the printing is never done, close to the edge of the frame, it is desired to coat lacquer in about one-half inch beyond the tape on the two sides and two inches beyond the tape on the two ends. This lacquer coat serves as sealer for the frame and inhibits spreading of ink to the corners.

(c) Base Board

For smooth and better printing, a base board is essential. A base board acts as a smooth surface on which to print and position the screen accurately onto the paper.

The base board should be smooth flat wood such as plywood etc. The base board should be larger than the screen. The screen is joined to the base board with a pair of hinges. During printing after each impression one has to lift the screen and insert sheets of paper or allied materials between the screen and base board. For smooth operation the screen printing tables are counter balanced so that the screen rises automatically after each impression.

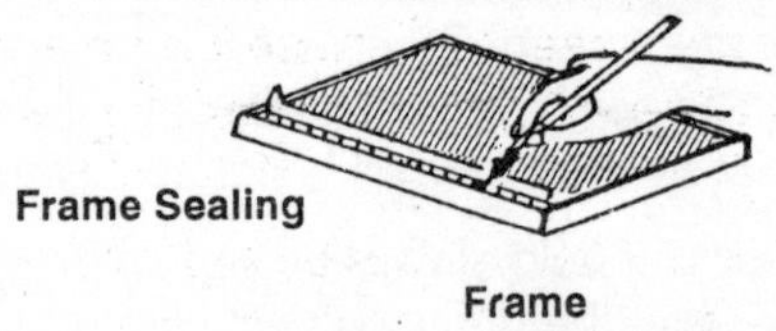

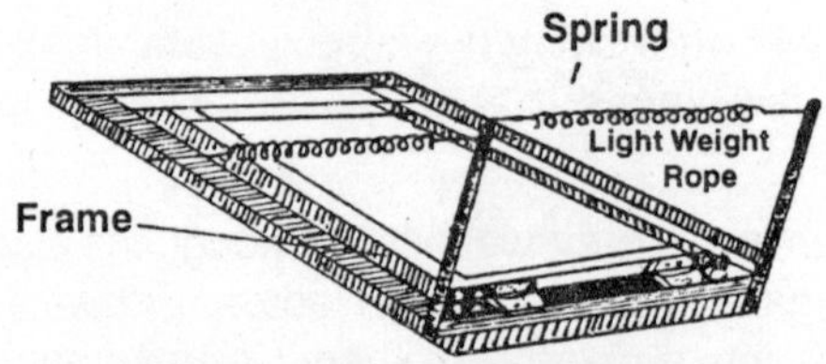

SIMPLE COUNTER BALANCE

(d) Squeegee, G-Clamps, Drying, Rack

Squeezee is a betting rubber, about 1 1/4" x 3/8", mounted in wood handle usually hard wood. It is used to force the ink through the open mesh of the stencil (Basin side).

The conventional screen printer uses a rubber blade approximately 7mm to 8mm thick mounted on a wooden handle. The rubber should have smooth edges to facilitate uniform penetration of ink through the mesh.

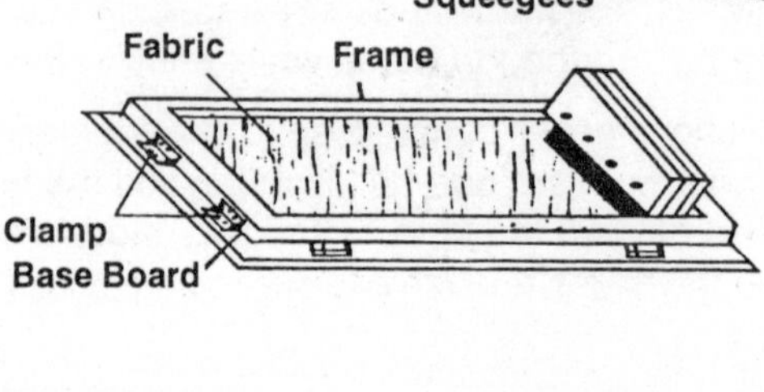

G-Clamps :

G-Clamps help the screen frame as firmly secured to the wooden strip. For larger size frames two G clamps may be used to obtain better firmness. These clamps are easily available in the market.

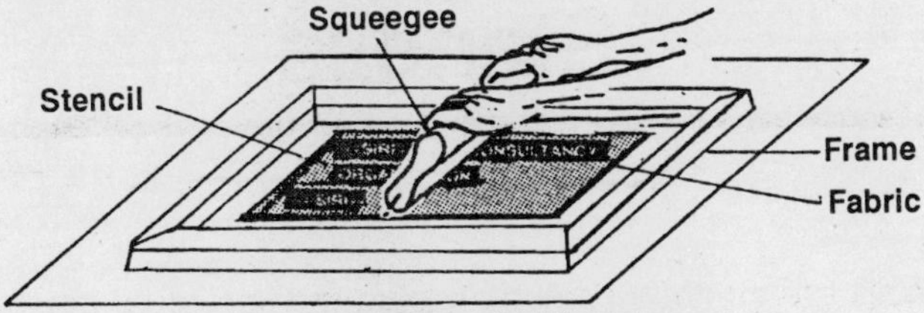

Hand Operated Squeegee

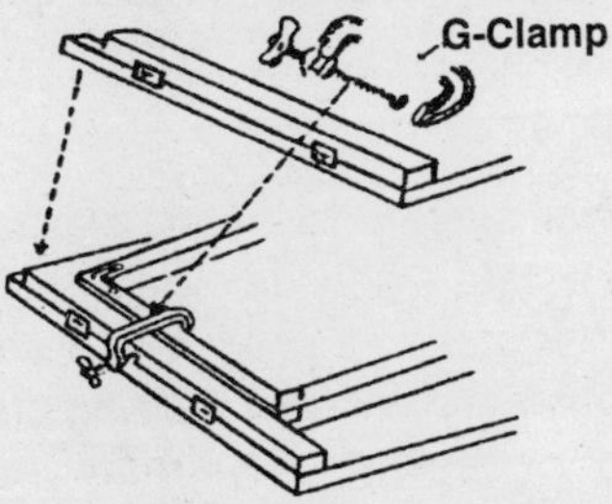

Drying Racks :

The printed matters required time to dry up completely. Suitable drying arrangements have to be made to keep the printed matters separate from one another. The drying racks occupy less space and are not so expensive. These drying racks are made from wooden batten. Cloth ribbons are fixed tightly by help of small nails in a parallel arrangement. These racks can be placed one over another.

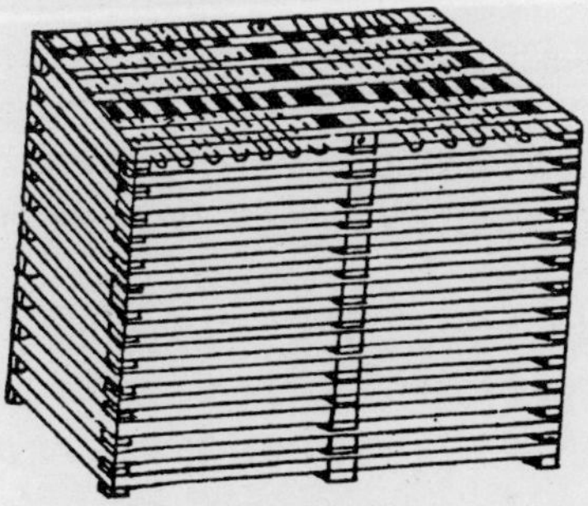

Drying Racks

8

Stencils

Stencils are stretched smoothly onto the screen or mesh and when ink is spread over it, and scrapped, the image is produced by blocking the pores in the screen in the non printing areas so no ink penetrates through these area.

(a) Paper Stencil

The paper stencil system is a fast, inexpensive way to print simple layouts such as real estate signs, sale banners, price tickets, posters etc. In comparison to other stencil it produces a sharp clean line. The paper stencils are very popular in rural area printing process due to their low cost and small amount of necessary preparation makes this ideal system to use when there are no small details in the design.

The lacquer type stencil films are now-a-days used throughout. Those are Ulanofilm, Nufilm, Profilm and Bhufilm etc.

In case of lacquer type stencil, a layer of lacquer is usually coated beneath the transparent sheet (waxed or polymer).

This mounting sheet serves as a temporary support for the stencil while being cut, packed and transferred to the silk. It holds all the pieces in the place.

Soon the stencil is pressed onto the screen the transparent sheet is removed. The lacquer layer gets stuck to the screen and form image area through which ink can penetrate. However it may be noted that paper stencils are used only for simple or rough work. Any way one can gain experience for perfect jobs.

Paper Stencil Cutting : The stencil cutting is an art and requires special skill to produce best possible stencil. The design is kept on drawing board and the corners are fixed by help of drawing pin or cellotape. The top side of the sheet (lacquer coated) is used to cut the stencil and enough care should be taken so that no impression of the cutting tool is produced on the baking sheet. The design to be produced on the sheet is clearly visible from the top as the sheet is transparent.

Stencil Cutting

By help of different stencil cutters such as adjustable compass cutter, bicutter and swinel cutter etc. a clear design can be made on the sheet.

Minimum pressure should be excerted on the cutting tool since more pressure on cutting tool may leave impression on the baking sheet.

Solvents such as Methyl ethyl ketone, Ethyl acetate, Butyl acetate are sprayed on the screen and the transfer sheet is (lacquered portion) pressed on to the screen. The binder part gets dissolved in the solvent and sticks to the screen. The lacquer film gets dried to the screen by evaporation of solvent.

It is very difficult to produce clear design by help of knife cut film screen and now-a-days the use of these types stencil is not encouraged.

AN UNUSUAL USE OF THE STENCIL TECHNIQUE SHOWN HERE IN A NINETEEN CENTURY AMERICAN BED SPREAD USING OIL PIGMENTS.

(b) Block Out Stencil

This type stencil is extensively used by screen printers. The only advantage of this method is easy to prepare it, and doesn't require any other separate stencil. But the drawback is rough type of printing. The image is not so clean and the sharpness is hindered.

The screen itself acts as stencil and the non image is created by coating with glue. The glue coated portion doesn't allow the ink to penetrate through the screen. The area not coated with glue, allows the ink to penetrate through the screen and finally forms the image.

The original design work is mounted onto the screen. It is important that the stencil should be bonded evenly without any wrinkles in the image making area, by help of transparent tapes.

Then by help of pencil the design is traced on the screen. These non image areas are sealed by help of glue, shellac or lacquers. Hence image area is left behind so the ink can pass out.

(c) Tusche Glue Stencil

Tusche is available in solid and liquid form. It is a kind of ink used for preparing tracing on special papers used by Offset printers. The design to be printed is stuck by its corners to the underside of the mesh, with help of gum tapes. Now the portions to be printed is filled in with Tusche. Thereafter hold it against source and check details. Undesirable tusche can be wiped off by help of turpentine oil. By help of a card board, coat the entire fabrics with a thin coat of glue. To ensure best result apply two coats. After perfect drying clean the underside, by turpentine keeping the frame vertical. Then repeat the same on reverse side also. After ensuring perfect drying, start printing.

(d) Shellac Stencil

Shellac stencil are extensively used for their inherent advantage over other types of stencil. Shellac stencil gives very sharp impression in case it is printed with flat and long gloss inks. It is mostly used for printing sign boards, hoardings, tin signs and banners. In case of paper stencil. It is impossible to cut design's which separates from the body, letters such as 'O', 'D' etc. In turn shellac stencils eliminates these short coming of paper stencil. Usually shellac stencil papers are available in sheets and wax coated. The design to be printed is kept as the base board (shellac side up). Positioning the design and shellac paper on the board have to be done by sticking with cellotape at the corners. One can take help of stencil cutter to cut out the design. The design is cut in such a manner that only the shellac paper is cut through not the baking sheet. One should cut and remove the shellac coating only from those areas of the design, which are required to printed and rest portion should be left intact. Pick up the shellac stencil paper and position it on the base board ensuring shellac side up. The screen is placed on the shellac stencil paper, so that is in perfect contact with the shellac stencil paper. Here one can put a folded cloth on the fabric, so the hot iron can be run over it, without damaging the mesh. One can take advantage of thermostat electric iron for the sais purpose.

Raise the frame slowly and remove the baking sheet gently. Therefore coat the unwanted areas with gum and dry it thoroughly. When the screen is thoroughly dry, it is ready for printing. After printing the shellac portions can be removed with methylated spirit. It would be better if little dye may be mixed in transparent glue, which would rather make it translucent, so that one can see better while working an small details.

The screen should not be dried in direct sun light. One can take help of table fan for effective drying. Soon after drying the screen is held against a source to ensure blocking out is perfect, leaving the image areas there should be no hole left behind. To ensure best result generally two coats of glue is applied onto the screen.

(e) Photographic Stencil

The photographic stencil has been an important factor in the steady advance made by screen printing. This stencil is used for designs and small letters etc. This produces a sharp impression. The function of this stencil is same as shellac stencil. In this case the photographic pigment gelatin is transferred to the screen by special exposing and development effects.

Positive : When a design or drawing is photographed, a negative copy of the original design is obtained. But in case of positive a faithful reproduction of the design is obtained and the image is not reversed as in case of negative.

(f) Pigment Paper Stencil

Pigment paper is a type of photographic paper coated with sensitive gelatin and is used extensively for photo stencils. The photographic stencil paper is extensively used in screen printing process, pigment paper is otherwise called carbon tissue, which comes in rolls.

A temporary sheet is produced by rubbing colourless shoe cream and spreading it over the celluloid or plastic sheet. This temporary support is prepared afresh every time cleaning the celluloid sheet with spirit.

(g) Sensitising Bath

Sensitising bath solution contains either Potassium bichromate or Ammonium bichromate. Usually 2 to 4% solution of Potassium bichromate or Ammonium bichromate is used (2% solution can be prepared by dissolving 50 gms of diluted potassium or ammonium bichromate in 2.5 litres of water).

The sensitising bath solution is taken in a tray. The pigment paper is immersed in bath and special care must be taken to cheek the curling of the paper at first. It can be avoided by gently rubbering the paper with your finger tips.

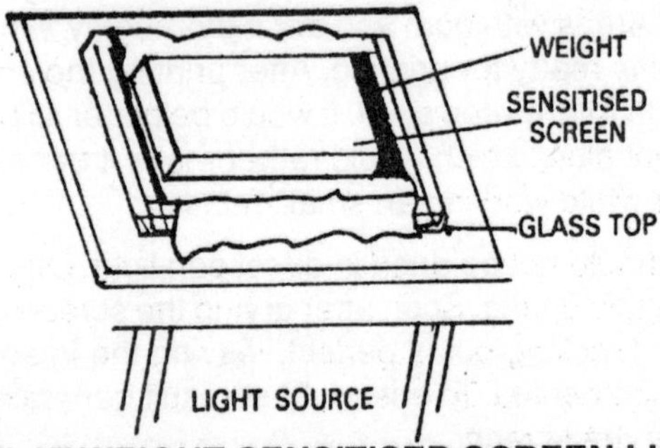

FLAT WEIGHT SENSITISED SCREEN LIGHT

To ensure satisfactory immersion and through sensitising, shake the tray gently. The dipping time is not more than two minutes. Then the paper is removed. The temporary support is kept on glass sheet. The pigment paper is then placed on the temporary support with the emulsion side against the waxed surface of the temporary support. By help of clean cloth the over spread sensitising solution is cleaned.

Precautions should be taken during sensitising and pressing the pigment paper onto the temporary support, these steps should be carried in absolutely dark place.

Next step is to clean both the sides of glass sheet of the photo exposing frame. The positive is placed on the top of the glass with the design or letter side up. Then the pigment paper is placed on the top of this positive paper, with temporary support side in direct contact with positive and the pigment paper backing side facing up. The photo exposing is shut tightly before exposing. The frame should be covered with black cloth and during exposure the cloth is removed. The timing for exposure depends upon the intensity of the available height as well on the density of the positive. The exposure time should be kept between 5 to 10 minutes in less bright sunlight and 2 to 4 minutes in bright sunlight. When the exposure time is over, the cloth is replaced and the frame is brought back to dark room.

If in case the pigment paper is under exposed then, gelatin layer will be thin and may not stand printing.

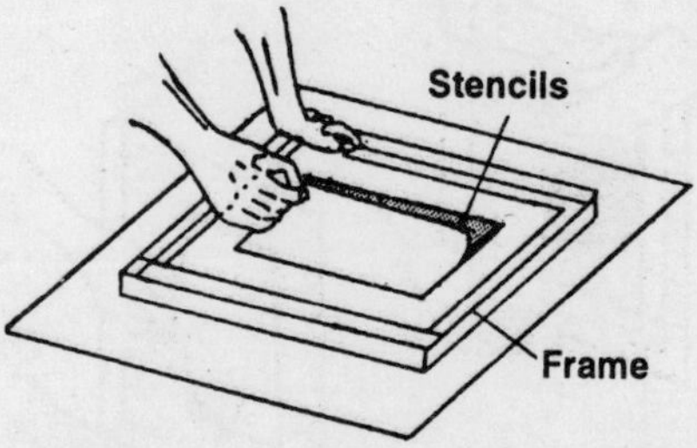

REMOVING FILM BACKING SHEET

On the other hand if the pigment paper is over exposed then the edges will be blurred and often becomes difficult to detach the support paper.

The frame is opened in the dark room. The temporary support and exposed pigment paper are removed from the frame. Then immersed in lukewarm water (45°C). Soon the paper baking is removed from the pigment paper and thrown away. The exposed pigment paper is shaked well in lukewarm water, by holding its corners. Unexposed layer of gelatin gets dissolved in water and turning the water brown in colour. The coloured water is thrown out and fresh water poured in. This process is repeated twice and then cold water is added to ensure that all unexposed gelatin comes off leaving the exposed gelatin stuck to the support paper.

This process lasts for 5 to 7 minutes and a clear sharp impression developed on the support paper.

(h) Precautionary Measures

1. During time of exposure the glass sheet may get heated and in turn might melt the gelatin of the pigment paper, so to avoid this a piece of ice may be rubbed over the glass sheet on the exposing frame.
2. The time of exposure must be fixed by hit and trial basis. The pigment paper should not be under or over exposed.
3. During handling the exposed pigment paper, enough care must be taken that your finger prints or any other marks should not come, during developing and washing pigment paper. Never rub the finger over the surface of exposed pigmented paper to hasten dissolving of the unexposed gelatin.

(i) Setting the Stencil onto the Screen

The stencil is kept on a sheet of glass, with gelatin side up. The screen fabrics placed right on the gelatin of the paper. Then a book or pile of new

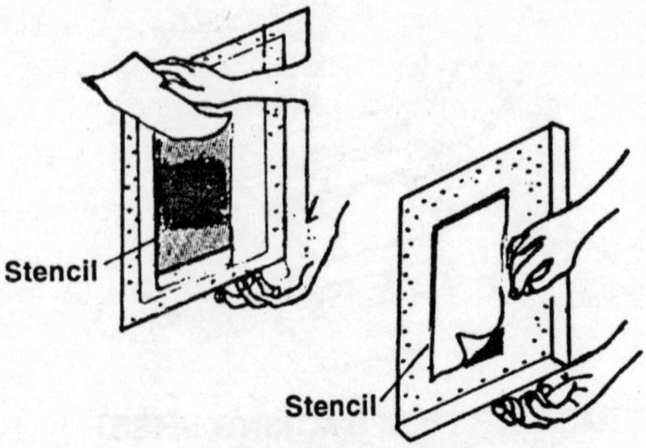

THE FILM STENCIL

papers are placed over the screen for a few minutes, so the stencil get stuck to the screen perfectly.

The support paper is removed slowly, starting from a corner where there is no gelatin. The exposed negative impression on the pigment paper has been transferred to the screen.

(i) Presensitised film stencils

A spectacular turn occurred in printing industries when presensitised film stencils came into the market. Now-a-days the use of paper stencil is very limited.

As from the name it appears, there is no need of sensitising the pigment paper and temporary support. Presensitised film stencils must be stored in dark room. These stencils are now available in local markets. There are two types of presensitised film stencils which are available in market.

The positive is taken and kept on exposing frame. The film is cut as to bit larger size than the positive and kept over the positive (the matt side should face the positive). The frame is shut and then exposed to direct sunlight. Care should be taken that film should not be over exposed. The exposed film is immersed in 20% hydrogen peroxide (hardener) and shaked for about a minute.

The film should be entirely immersed and no part should left out. The hardener makes the exposed portions stiff and do not allow them to get dissolved during washing.

The film is taken out and kept over a clean glass plate, matt side up. The glass plate is immersed along with film in luke warm water (45°C) bath and shaked for one minute. The glass plate is then kept at 45° angle and luke warm water is poured from the top. The unexposed part goes into water and exposed image will stand clear. This process is repeated till sharpness is obtained.

The glass plate alongwith film is kept on the base plate and the screen is then placed over the film. Either the plate or the screen should be displaced from the set position. Excess water which might come up through the mesh, should be caitiously and highly blotted out with a new sprint.

The film is left to dry properly under a fan. After one hour, the backing sheet is peeled off cautiously by the corners only. (The baking sheet will readily come off by slight peeling, when the film is complete dry). Now the unit is ready for printing.

(k) Precautionary measures :

1. Hardener is kept in dark place in dark coloured bottles. The film should be immersed in hardener matt side up.
2. Once the screen is kept over the glass plate, the position should not change under any circumstances.
3. The frame should not be dried under direct sun light.

These presensitised film is available in the market in the name of 5 star film and Ulano film.

(l) Sensitising the screen

Specialized industrial applications of the process as for example textile, which takes the advantage of using presensitising the screen directly due to nature of printing, these screens have to be large in size and textile mill find it convenient to sensitise the screen.

The screen is coated in a light sensitive emulsion, which hardens when exposed to light. The screen fabric is stretched by one type of stretching device or it can also done by manually. The lacquer or adhesive is then coated onto the top surface of the screen frame and left to dry. The pattern to be produced is painted on transparent paper with dense opaque ink. In fact for multicolour design separate painting and screen is necessary.

The positive (painted pattern) is placed in contact with sensitised screen and exposed to day light.

The screen is washed clear in water and allowed to dry thoroughly.

(m) Coating the screen

The sensitising solution or light sensitive emulsion consist of either of the two.

(A) 30 gms of poly vinyl alcohol or 30 cms of photographic gelatin and dissolve it in 255 ml of water and keep it in ready stock.

Again dissolve 10 gms of potassium or ammonium bichromate in 100 ml of water and keep it in dark colour bottle.

The powders are charged slowly and under constant stirring. The poly vinyl alcohol or photographic gelatin dissolved in water is taken in inner pot and the outer pot is filled with water and kept over low fire. The bichromate solution is poured in and stirred constantly to avoid lumps formation.

At this stage it is necessary to add few drops of glycerine to make the solution easy to apply onto the fabrics.

The container is taken off and solution is poured to a separate vessel.

This emulsion may be applied with a flat, semi soft brush. As the layer is not light sensitive while wet, the coating may be done in diffused light. The screen is kept at 45° angle and metal angle squeezes can be used, because too thin a layer is often applied with metal edge.

Screens are dried under a fan in a dark room immediately after coating. After drying the screen is coated again on the reverse side.

It is not advisable to expose the film to direct sunlight because a large frame is required to fit the screen frame inside it. It would be economical to expose the screen to artificial light which does not require such a large frame.

The distance between source and the frame should be such that screen is evenly exposed to light. The positive is placed on the glass and the corners are fixed by help of cellotape.

The sensitised screen frame is kept over the positive in such a manner that the mesh is evenly in contact with positive. To avoid shifting of position, a heavy weight is kept over the frame.

Ensuring perfect position of the frame, the screen is then exposed to light for desired time (by trial basis). The whole set up (frame) is immersed in a large tray containing lukewarm water. The exposed portions hardens and unexposed portions of the coating goes into the solution.

The process is repeated till unexposed portion of the coating must be washed out completely. A sharp and clear image appears on the screen after subsequent washing. The washing time should be between 3 to 4 minutes. The screen is taken out and dried before a fan. After ensuring thorough drying the screen is taken and checked for pin-holes. The pin-holes are blocked out by help of soft brush with emulsion.

The edges of the screen frame are reinforced by fixing adhesive tape round the inner edges of frame. To ensure better result usually lacquer is coated. Now the screen is ready for use.

(n) Important Notes

1. Exposure time : The time of exposing should be as follow for sensitized solution.

   (a) Sunlight (Direct) 16 - 20 seconds
   (b) Sunlight (Cloudy) 20 - 25 seconds
   (c) Metal halide (5000 Watts) 40 - 25 minutes

2. Ensure perfect contact is made between positive and the solution of the screen. One can take help of a piece of glass or steel.

3. Emulsion side up positive in case of direct printing. But not in case of transfer printing.

4. Clear yarn screen before coating, by detergent powder.

5. Coat both sides of screen for better result.

6. Never use heavy spray when washing the fabric.

9

Chemicals Used and Formulations

(1) Ammonium Dichromate or Bichromate :

Orange needles, soluble in water and alcohol. Specific gravity– 2.152. It is used for sensitising. Generally 2 to 4% solution of ammonium dichromate is used. Stored in dark coloured bottle in cool dark place.

(2) Drier :

It is a chemical additive, which has power to accelerate the drying. Mostly cobalt, manganese lead compounds are used.

(3) Gelatin :

It is a type of protein obtained from collagen by boiling skin, ligament, bones etc. Type A gelatin is obtained from acid treated raw materials. Type B is obtained from alkali treated raw materials. Gelatin is used in pigment papers and stencils preparation.

(4) Glue :

Colloidal suspension of various protainaceous materials. It is used in screen printing for various purposes.

(5) Hydrogen Peroxide :

It is a colourless heavy liquid and sold in aqueous solution of various strengths. It is soluble in water and alcohol.

It is used as hardener for presensitised film. Hydrogen peroxide solution of twenty volumes strengths and is readily available. It is kept in dark place and in dark brown coloured bottles.

(6) Poly Vinyl Alcohol :

It is a water soluble synthetic polymer made by A alcoholysis of polyvinyl acetate. It is white to cream colour powder.

It is used along with bichromates for sensitising the screen directly. General 30 gms of P.V.A. is dissolved in 225 ml litres of cold water is used for the said purpose.

(7) Potassium Dichromate :

It is also called potassium bichromate. It is bright, yellowish red transparent crystal. Soluble in water, insoluble in alcohol.

It is used for sensitising bath solution. Generally 2 to 4% of potassium dichromate is recommended for the said purpose.

Stored in dark coloured bottle in cool dark place away from light.

(8) Reducer :

It is generally added to the ink to increase the working properties and flow of the ink. The viscosity of the ink is reduced by amyl acid. This also helps in cleaning the inks.

(9) Turpentine Oil :

Colourless liquid, penetrating odour, Immiscible with water. It is used as solvent and cleaning purposes.

(10) Hydroquinone :

White crystals soluble in water, alcohol and ether. Available in two grades technical and photographic. It is used as photographic developer (except colour film).

(11) Sodium Sulphite :

White crystals or powder, soluble in water and sparingly in alcohol. Used as photographic developer.

(12) Sodium Carbonate :

Grayish white powder or lumps Soluble in water and insoluble in alcohol.

(13) Potassium Bromide :

White crystalline granules or powder soluble in water and glycerin. Used in photography (gelatin bromide papers and plates).

(14) Glycerin :

Clear colourless syrupy liquid. Soluble in water and alcohol. Used as solvent and emulsifying agent.

FORMULATIONS

(a) Hydroquinone carbonate developer

Ingredients	*Parts by wt.*
Hydroquinone	20
Sodium Sulphite	150
Sodium Carbonate	50
Potassium Bromide	10
Water	2000 c.c.

This is a single solution developer used undiluted and is used to develop the positive.

Time of development	5 minutes
Temperature	20° C

Condition of processing-In dark room fitted with red safe light.

(b) Emulsion coating

Ingredients	*Parts by wt.*
Gelatin	90
Potassium Dichromate	20
Sodium Carbonate	2
Glycerine	7.5
Water	1000 c.c.

Potassium dichromates makes gelatin light sensitive and glycerin inhibits the cracks. Sodium carbonate reduces the acidity.

(c) Sensitising Solutions

Mostly the sensitising solutions are based on gelatin and poly vinyl alcohol, these are sensitised by either ammonium or potassium dichromate.

Formulation-1

(A) Dissolve 126 parts of gelatin in 553 parts of water at 60°C with stirring.

(B) Dissolve 51 parts of zinc oxide in 200 parts of water.

(C) Mix 14 parts of ammontium dichromate and 7 parts of potassium dichromate.

(D) Mix 50 parts of ammonia and 2.5 parts of calsolene Oil (Sulfated ester).

Then add Solution (B) to Solution (A) and slowly add C followed by D. Filter the mixture and coat the screen with this solution at 45-50°C. Allow to dry at room temperature in the dark.

Formulation-2

(A) Dissolve 95 parts of gelatin in 866 parts of water at 55-60°C with stirring.

(B) Then add 13.5 parts of ammonium dichromate followed by 20 parts of ammonla. At the end, add 3.5 parts of vegetable oil.

Filter this, then coat the screen with this solution at 50°C. Allow to dry at room temperature in dark.

(d) Solutions used for Hardening of the exposed Design

More often screen based on a gelatin dichromate sensitising solution are often given a hardening treatment. The screen itself washed or treated in the cold for 10-12 minutes in following solutions :

Formulation-1

Ingredients	*Parts by weight*
Ammonium Bichromate	25
Chrome Alum Crystals	50
Formaldehyde (40%)	50

This solution is bulked to 1000 parts.

After treatment the screen is washed with water and set to dry. In case Poly Vinyl Alcohol - dichromate sensitising solution is used then screen should be treated with following formulation for 45 minutes.

Formulation-2

Ingredients	*Parts by wt.*
Acetaldehyde	50
Normal Butyraldehyde	50
Sulphuric Acid	20

This solution is bulked to 1000 parts.

After treatment, the screen is washed and dried.

10
Common Faults in Screen Printing

(A) Ink Troubles

(a) Collection of Dirt : Spots, specks and filling in appear on the print, while dirt and coating may collect on the fabric.

Cause : (i) Ink drier too viscous
(ii) Ink film too tacky
(iii) Poor stock coating

(b) Fading of Colour : Heat sensitive pigments are mostly responsible for fading of colour during printing.

Cause : (i) Use of heat sensitive pigments
(ii) Use of liquid cobalt driers

(c) Filling of the Ink : When tiny solid loops fill up with ink and other closed areas appear as solid blobs on the print.

Cause : (i) Inks is too tacky, and is causing tiny specks of coating to deposit on the screen.
(ii) Screen filling is more often due to formation of skin or dry ink. Some times the particle accumulating in the dust.

(d) Insufficient Gloss : More often the ink penetrates into the stock and leaves a dull print.

Cause : (i) Medium is too thin.
(ii) Ink is too slow drying

(e) Mottling : This is very common defect found in case of printing ink. Mottling is confluent blotches of colour due to uneven distribution of ink on the surface of the substrate.

Cause : (i) Ink film too thick
(ii) Substrate is very hard
(iii) Ink too oily or too large
(iv) First layer crystallizes in case of two coats
(v) Low ink pigmentation.

(B) Troubles in case of Screen Making

(a) Pinholing : This is a type of defect where the appearance of fine, pimply elevation or tiny holes occur in the gelatin or poly vinyl alcohol/ dichromate film.

Cause : (i) Uneven distribution of sensitising solution
(ii) Dirt deposition on the screen
(iii) Very humid condition during application

(b) Washing out of exposed gelatin film.

Cause : (i) The film is under exposed
(ii) Exposed to very humid atmospheric conditions
(iii) Sensitising solution heated to high temperature.

(c) More often in some cases the exposed gelatin or P.V.A. dichromate film not completely removed from unexposed places.

Cause : (i) Film over exposed
(ii) Surrounding temperature is high
(iii) The positive film is not completely opaque.

(d) In some cases the design has poor edges.

Cause : (i) The screen is not in perfect contact with the positive.
(ii) The coating is too thick.

(e) Uneven distribution of coating.

Cause : (i) Dirt and grease are deposited on the fabric before coating.

11

Printing Unit

The basic printing equipment have already been discussed before. The whole printing set up is shown below.

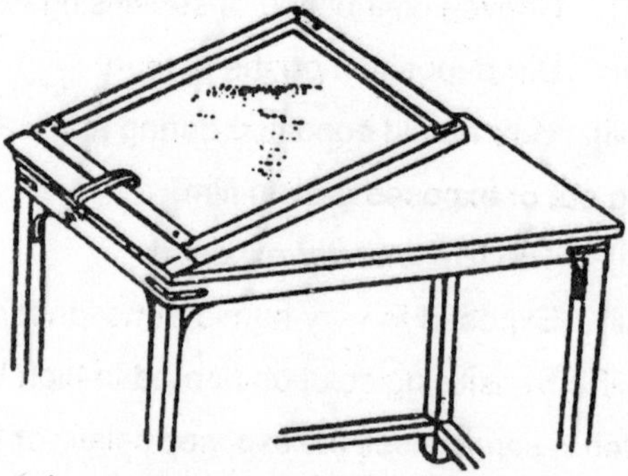

SCREEN PRINTING TABLE

Before you start printing it is worthwhile sorting out the workspace into "clean" and "unclean" areas. One should be careful in placing the blank sheets of paper or substrate in exact position. For proper positioning of paper one can use four. "Layworks" made by sticking short lengths of gum strips on to the base board. These gum strips prevent the paper from moving, as soon as the screen is closed. False inpression can be taken on blank paper so as to get fair idea of correct position of the paper in relation to stencil.

(a) How to Start Actual Printing

1. First ensure that stencil has stuck to the screen properly.
2. Then check, the stencil should be free from pinholes.
3. Leaving the printing remaning, remaining part of the screen should be blocked out either by lacquer or glue.

4. The frame must be set absolutely flat on the base plate.
5. "Lay marks" are properly set on the base board.
6. The fabric should jump away from substrate as the squeegee passes.
7. The edge of the squeegee should be smooth and free from dust.

Selection of ink is very important and it solely depends on the type of substrate or material to be printed. The desired shade is considered to match the colour of original design. Alternatively of one can mix two or three inks to counter upon the desired shade.

The material is kept on the base plate and frame is lowered to lie flat on the material or substrate. This is poured slowly on the hinged side of the frame and slightly away from the stencil. Avoid over spreading of inks and inks must be spread on confined area, almost near to stencil.

The squeegee is cleaned and dipped in that ink. The squeeze slowly pulled across, with slight pressure at 45° angle to the screen. The squeezee is pulled right across the stencil to the other end of the screen.

The squeegee is taken out and the frame lifts up by spring action.

The printed sheet or water is removed and process is repeated to print subsequently.

(b) Multi Colour Printing : The foremost advantage of screen printing is that it lends itself extremely well to multicolour printing. The process permits over printing of lighter shades over a dark background. It is often necessary to print a slightly thicker layer of second print to obliterate the first colour. If possible to achieve four to five colour printing when the colours on the design do not tend to overlap each other.

Multi colour printing is possible by just blocking out rest areas with transparent tapes. In case the colours in orginal design tend to overlap one another, it is advisable to make separate positives for each colour.

It should alway be kept in mind that for obtaining the desired shade you have to mix the inks and match it with exact shade. More often you have to mix two or more inks to bring out the desired tint.

Precautions to be taken during printing

1. Pour sufficient ink to maintain the flow. At first you will require much more ink and once you have good film of ink over the area you require, then very little ink is needed to print.

2. Uniform pressure must be applied at 45° angle to the screen, so as to avoid indistinct impression.

3. Do not pull the squeegee twice over the same sheet, otherwise second impression of the ink may spread out to undesirable areas.
4. Quality of the print is better if the fabric jumps away from the paper or material to be printed. It is desirable to keep the screen about 5 mm above the sheet. This gap is called "Snap Distance".
5. The excess ink should be removed with a rag dipped in kerosene from undesirable areas on the underside of the screen.

Cleaning the Screen

If you wish to reuse the screen you should keep it as clear as possible. Soon you have finished up printing clear the squeegee and screen with white sprit. (The stencil duplicator inks are soluble in white spirit).

When most of the ink is off, then wash off the stencil with water. If sufficient water is available then one can squirt a high pressure jet at the fabric without damaging it and this is effective way of removing waste matter.

12

Automatic Screen Printing Machine

The genesis of the printing industry can be traced back roughly to thousand years back. However, it developed in real sense only in eighteenth century. It gained momentum only few decades back due to very versatile process and effective also. Moreover the increasing expansion in screen printing applications calls for new solutions to most varied and often contrasting requirements such as perfect reproduction of works of art, accurate printing register for printed circuits as well as the standard production of screen printed designs on sturdily built and low priced machines.

Spectacular turn occurred when semi automatic and automatic screen printing machines came into the market. Anyhow before the advent of fully automatic screen printing machines a number of attempts had been made to partially mechanise some of the operations and so increase the output. The screen is raised and lowered and the squeegee is pulled across the screen automatically, the material to be printed has to be inserted and removed by hand in case of semi automatic screen printing.

The fully automatic presses also feed and deliver the printed paper automatically. Moreover in few cases an impression cylinder is attached which holds the paper while the screen moves in unison and the squeegee remains stagnant. Automatic screen printing set up is shown below.

Usually a vacuum base helps to separate the paper from the screen after the operation. To the vacuum pump, a flat piece of plastic laminate with regular spaced holes is connected.

In fact the paper is laid on a levelled surface with perforated base. The vacuum holds the paper flat. The screen frame is pulled down onto the

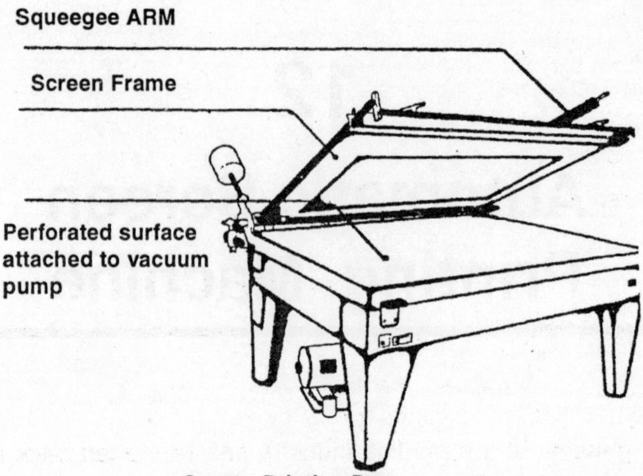

Screen Printing Press

substrate and squeegee is automatically pulled across to force the ink to pass faithfully through the fabrics in the image areas of the screen into the substrate.

For effective drying in case of semi automatic and automatic machines often have drying tunnels or ultraviolet drying units.

The electromechanically driven, semi automatic machine, easy to use and of simple construction, enables the operator to set up with minimum expense a screen printing laboratory where accurate prints can be obtained at low cost per unit.

The printing top is made of light weight metal alloy. In fact over the printing top number of holes connected to a powerful motor exhaust. The vacuum on the printing top is created by a high power and noiseless built-in motor exhaust, which is actuated automatically at the beginning of each printing cycle when the frame lowers and disengaged when the frame rises. Three controls fitted on the front and side part of the machine allow for accurate register by means of longitudinal, transversal and rotational movements of printing top. Once the registration has been accomplished the top is locked into position.

The frame carriage is fitted on the back of the machine with book-type opening and allows frames with different formats to be inserted. The smallest frame size in the printing direction is approx 57 cms. More often a special device fitted to the front bar of the frame carriage prevents unwanted side movements of the screen during printing thus ensuring perfect register. The squeegee and scraper speed can be infinitely adjusted by means of a lever. During the printing stroke the squeegee exerts pressure on the stet of the stroke the squeegee rises and the scraper lowers thus coming into contact with the fabric. Thus during the return stroke the scraper forces the ink backwards flooding the mesh for the subsequent print.

In turn the squeegee and scraper pressure on the fabric can be adjusted even during the printing cycle by special fitted screws.

Interestingly the squeegee angle can be adjusted to obtain excellent results with fine detailed line printing. Same way printing stroke can also be continuously adjusted by means of a lever fitted on the back of machine.

Moreover the automatic "off contact" allows a gradual separation of the fabric from the printed substrate after the squeegee has passed on. This particular device allows the printer to print solid areas without halo effects even with fine detailed reverse printing.

13

Screen Printing on Different Surfaces

Every operator appreciates the advantage of screen printing that it is very versatile and very versatile and very effective process if used appropriately on any substrate, regardless of size and shape. This is only process which can be used for printing from paper to nuclear reactors. Needless to say, there is virtually no such material which cannot be printed by help of this process.

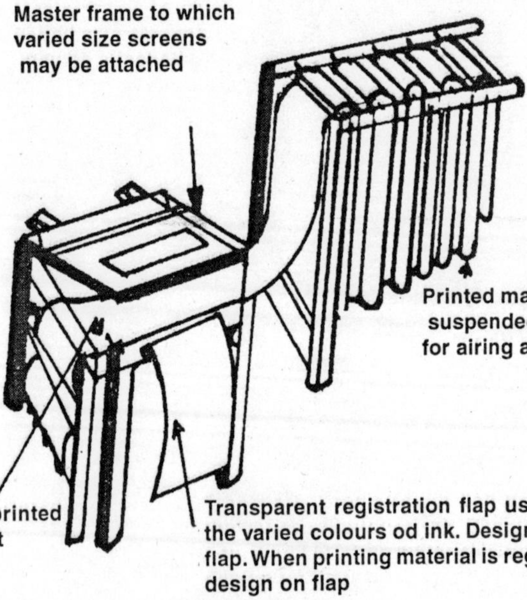

TEXTILE PRINTING

The most significant contribution of the century to textile printing development has been hand screen printing. It is the only process that has so changed the character of design in fashion and furnishing fabrics all over the world.

The substrates available for printing are of wide range such as glass, walls, vehicles, machinery, furnitures, ceramics etc. These can be broadly grouped as absorbent and non absorbent surfaces. In case of non absorbent substrates like glass, plates, metal sheet etc, stiffer ink has to be spread with more pressure and image is much sharper. On the other hand image is dull in case of absorbent substrates, like paper, jute bags, porous materials.

(a) **Paper and Card :** The screen printing process can be used to print on variety of papers and cards. The wide range of paper such as blotting paper, hand made paper, bond paper, kraft paper and metallic paper such as silver, golden etc. The composition of ink should be such that it holds well to the substrate. Mostly oil based inks are used to reduce brittleness upon drying. In fact P.V.C. and Fluorecent inks are also used for printing on cards and papers.

(b) **Glass Surface :** The glass piece is cleaned by help of caustic soda or washing powder. Ensure that the glass sheet is free from dust, grease and oil marks. The sharp edges and corners of the glass sheets should be rounded off. Otherwise the screen will be frayed by the sharp edges. The printing is done on the back of a glass sheet or sign, the sequence of colours should be reversed and inturn the letterings, should be printed in reverse so that it will read correct from front side.

(c) **Plastics :** Screen printing can be done on variety of plastic substrates immaterial of size and shape. In this case silk screen P.V.C. inks are used to get better grip on plastic objects. On variety of substrates made of poly vinyl chloride, melamine crokery, thermowares, expanded polystyrene, polypropylene film auto parts, caprolactum gears, plastic jugs, plastic shoes, soles etc. In case of cellophane sheets, it often difficult to handle them and register accurately against the guides. Normally the cellophane sheet is mounted on card board by help of gum tapes at the corner. So that during printing operation the object is not move away from the exact image area.

(d) **Tin Plates :** The tin plates are cleaned thoroughly to remove dirt, grease etc. A clear or lacquer coating is done on tin plates by help of spray gum or brush. Then left it to dry completely. The screen fabric is reinforced for extra protecting during printing. Mostly glossy or semi glossy inks are used for printing on tin plates.

(e) **Jute Bags and Cloth Banners :** These are absorbant surfaces and sharpness of printing should not be expected on such surfaces. The jute or ordinary coarse cloth is kept on the printing table using gum spots or cellotape at the corners. Single colour is used as multi colour job registration is impossible on such porous substrates. In turn printing on long banners is normally done in a single colour and printed in ports as adjustable to the printing top. For excellent prints, one should get the banner stretched and smoothly ironed. So irregular shapes and wrinkles may not obstruct the final printing. One can take advantage of drawing pin or gum tapes to fix the banner to ensure exact position.

14

Inks for Screen Printing

Screen printing inks have specific characteristic such as they should pass faithfully through the openings without clogging and dry quickly on the printed matter.

The ascending progress has been the result principally of mechanical and intensive amount of research work which is now being done compared to that of decades ago. The fruits of this research work have resulted in developing "Synthetic Inks". These synthetic inks dry by evaporation leaving behind a thin opaque film. There are so many types of inks available in the market, suitable for variety of surfaces, drying mat, semi-mat or glossy.

These are inks used for screen printing are different for different substrates as below :

(a) On advertising posters
(b) On card and paper
(c) On P.V.C., metal, canvas, plastics and fabrics
(d) On gum tapes
(e) On tin plates and thick metal sheets
(f) On glass and ceramics
(g) In textiles
(h) On curved surface such as vases and bottles
(i) On cloth banners and jute bags

Nature of Ink

The screen inks should be short, so that it drags on, the squeegee does not occur and clear impression can be obtained. Ink should pass faithfully through the screen and

The screen inks should run over the screen easily, without much pressure and pass through without causing blur. The consistency of the inks should not be too high or low. If high then results in stringing and hairy impressions. If low then causes flooding and blurred edges.

On drying the ink must form a continuous film free of residual tack and other defects.

Screen printing ink is a dispersion of pigments in medium which are, for the most part, solution or resins in solvents. These inks dry by evaportion of solvent and in some cases it is a combination of oxidation and evaporation. The main resins used are rosin esters, phenolics, cellulose dervative, vinyls and oleo-resinuous varnishes. The choice of binder system soley depend on the film properties desired.

(a) Manufacturing of Screen Printing Inks : The pigments are mixed with vehicle to produce a low viscous paste and rest ingredients such as solvents, dries, dispersing aid are added. The ingredients are mixed by help of heavy duty mixers such as dough mixers, pony mixers. The primary mixings partially wets the pigments but simultaneuosly forms agglomerate mass of semi wetted pigment. After thorough mixing in the mixer the paste is fed to the roller mills. These mills contains 3 to 5 rolls and speed of the rolls are different. In case of 3 roll mill the middle roll is fixed. The material from the last roll is scrapped by help of scrappers. In three roll mills the pigment and vehicle mixture is thoroughly grinded and dispersed. The pigment vehicle mixture is in semi viscous form for better grinding and dispersion. After the mixture is grounded the properly solvents are added to make it ready mixed product. This thing is done in turbo mixers or ordinary mixers. These turbo mixers contains a shaft to which paddle shaped rotors are attached. These are slow speed mixers usually employed for thinning and proper tinting of different shades. Then the finished products are packed.

Important

1. Choice of proper solvents for screen printing process.
2. The solvent should not react with the substrate and medium.
3. Pigment volume concentration should be taken into consideration for better gloss.
4. Proper care must be taken so that the ink should not dry on the roll mills. The drier should not react with medium or pigment.
5. Selection of suitable ink for a particular substrate.

The screen printing process can apply a thick film of ink to the substrate than other printing processes. The manufacturers take the advantages where maximum capacity is desired, or where fluorescent pigments are used, or for printing P.C.B (Printed Circuit Board).

Screen printing process can be used for various substrates such as card boards, art paper, metal signs, glass, cermics, plastics, tin containers and leather. According to substrate the types of printing inks vary. The ink during manufacture is formulated for a particular type of substrate. One can take advantage by using particular ink which is specified for a particular substrate. The desired property depends on selection of vehicle. In this case one have to select the oils, resins, solvents, driers and additives.

The Important aspects considered

(a) Nature of substrate (paper, plastics, metal sheets, glass etc.)
(b) Whether air drying or stoving type
(c) Atmospheric exposure conditions.
(d) Gloss desired for the particular job.
(e) Special requirement as proposed by customer.

Needless to say for selecting the vehicle, which will impart the desired properties, one should bring into mind the properties of resin, oils solvents, driers and additives to blend then as required by final formulations.

(b) Classification of Screen Process Inks

(1) Oil based Inks : In this oil based inks, oil acts as the binder and controls the film properties. The film property also depends on the net oil content and whether oil is drying or non drying.

In all types of inks containing drying oils, the essential drying after application to form a hard insoluble decorative impression is mainly due to chemical changes which takes place in oil on exposure to the atmosphere. This oil based inks are mostly used for printing paper, wood, fabrics, leathers etc.

These oil based inks are also known as silk screen inks S.S. Inks. These oil based inks are available in various forms such as semi glossy, matt, glossy, egg shell, according to pigment volume concentration (P.V.C.).

(2) Nitrocellulose Screen Inks :– These are expensive than oil based screen inks but posses several added advantages. Nitrocellulose provides media of suitable viscosity. Nitrocellulose inks are fast drying and still then allow the ink to remain, sufficiently wet in the screen to avoid clogging. By suitable formulation a very transparent ink can be prepared.

Is has few drawbacks also which are costly, fire hazardous, toxic in nature (due to solvents). Nitrocellulose inks can be suitably used on variety of substrates like, wood, paper, plastics, leather, metal parts, glass etc.

(3) Screen Inks for P.V.C. : The screen inks for printing on plastic surfaces generally consists of a vehicle composed of a drying synthetic resin dissolved in linseed, perilla or tungoil. Mostly modified phenolics and hard drying alkyds are used.

The great care must be taken doing choice of pigment since the hard drying synthetic resins have high acid values and may react with basic pigment.

Earlier a suitable type of ink was formulated for P.V.C., which was based on P.V.C. powder resin dissolved in solvent and pigmented with titanium dioxide. Although the finish is matt since the pigment volume concentration is above 60% but adhesion to most of P.V.C. sheeting is excellent.

If solvents like toluene is used then properties like adhesion, flexibility hardness increases for use on polytheylene sheets. In case if cyclohexanone is used then said properties increases for use on P.V.C. Sheets.

(4) Fluorescent Inks : Fluorescence is a type of luminescence which a atom or molecule emit visible radiattion in passing from higher to a lower electronic state. When light source falls on fluorescent inks it results in excellent lurid appearance.

Mostly fluorescent inks contain the radio-excired materials like Colloidal Zinc, Barium, Strontium and Calcium Sulphides.

A fluorescent ink can be made by dissolving anthracene and rubber in benzene, and adding sulphur chloride to the solution to vulcanize the rubber after printing.

Fluorescent dyes can be manufactured by dissolving fluorescent dystuffs in a fused melamine sulphonamide/formaldehyde resin, which is then allowed to cool. Then the pulverised coloured resin is grounded into suitable medium. The fluorescent inks can be used on various surfaces such as paper, leather, plastics, and metal sheets to create a lurid appearance.

(5) Catalysed Screen Inks : Catalysed screen inks possess many advantages like outstanding durability, excellent adhesion to different substrates, good gloss, excellent resistance to solvents, water, chemicals, abrasives etc.

The catalysed inks are supplied in two packs and usually stoved to bring their special properties. Ink is based on epoxy system and are mixed with required quantity of catalyst ("Proprietory basis") supplied by the ink manufacturers. The mixing of catalyst should be one hour before the use. If detained for prolonged period then the properties deteriorates. Interestingly the films are screen printed as thin as possible to get maximum adhesion and sharpness.

(6) Stoved Screen Inks : These stoved screen inks can be satis factorily used for printing metal, polyethene, poly vinyl chloride (P.V.C.), glass, kadin, porecelain etc.

These inks have to be formulated faithfully pass through the screen and print, then dry with the stoving schedule. In turn these inks as a class have superior hardness, adhesion, flexibility, durability and good resistance properties.

Needless to say much harder film can be obtained by stoving the print in an electric oven for 10-15 minutes at 80-120°C.

Formulations of Screen Printing Inks

1. Oil Based Screen Printing Inks

Ingredients	*% by weight*
Long Oil Alkyd	15
Colour	2
Cobalt Napthenate	1
M.T.O.	22
Calcium Carbonate	60

2. Oil Based Screen Inks for Poster

Ingredients	*% by weight*
Chrome Red	14
Calcium Carbonate	31
Blanc Fix	34
Stand Oil (Viscosity 100 Poise)	11
White Spirit	10
Cobalt Napthenate (6%)	0.2
Manganese Napthenate (6%)	0.2

3. P.V.C. Sheeting Ink

Ingredients	*% by weight*
Poly Vinyl Chloride	10
Vinyl/Vinylidene Chloride Copolymer	10
Pigment	6
Cylclohexnonyl Phthalate	4
Methyl Isobutyl Ketone	10
Isomeric Methyl Cyclohexanones	60

4. Inks for P.V.C. (i)

Ingredients	*% by weight*
White Pigment (Titanium Dioxide)	20
Kaolin	2
Cyclohexanonyl Phthalate	3
Vinylite Resin	12
Isomeric Dimethyl Cyclohexanone	13
Isomeric Methyl Cyclohexanone	50

(ii)

Ingredients	*% by weight*
Polyvinyl Resin	50
Cyclohexanone	100
Methyl Ethyl Ketone	20
Dibutyl Phthalate	5
Phthalocynine Green	20
Toluidene Red	6.5
Calcium Carbonate	30
Titanium Dioxide	20

5. Inks for Ceramic Substrates

Ingredients	*% by weight*
Potassium Carbonate	1
Borax	1
Lead Oxide	2
Cobalt Nitrate	2

All ingredients are mixed with raw linseed oil with possibly a little turpentine oil.

6. Bright Blue Ink

Ingredients	*% by weight*
Prussian Blue	10
Titanium Dioxide	2
Gloss White	18
Alumina Hydrate	3
Varnish & Drier	67

15

Adhesives

Glue is used for attaching cellophone for oil colour processing only. ¾ lb. of gum arabic powder is dissolved in one quart of water. After straining, 1½ lbs., of glycerine and 1/8 ounce formaldehyde are added. This solution is applied to the cellophone with brush and while it is tacky the cellophone paper is attached to the screen.

Celluloid adhesives *(inflammable)*

1. Celluloid 1 part, acetone 3 parts, amyl acetate 2 parts mix, dissolve and add ½ part of castor oil.
2. Celluloid 1 part, camphor 1 part, alchohol 5 parts.
3. Celluloid 5 parts, camphor 2 parts, sulphuric ether 10 parts, acetone 10 parts.
4. Celluloid 1 ounce, gum sandarac 1 oz. castor oil 5 drops.
5. Celluloid 1 oz., castor oil 7 drops.
6. Shellac 1 part, spirit of camphor 1 part, alchohol 2 parts – dissolve in warm and apply while hot.
7. Prepared film cements, patented.
8. Celluloid solvents are acetone, sulphuric ether, amyl acetate, oil of turpentine, alchohol, etc. Solvent made of one part of amyl acetate and acetone each and ¼ of benzol or naptha is also useful.

Profilm

Profilm is transparent number or blue coloured gelatin-like sheet of film composed of two layers held together, upper one used as stencil and the lower one as backing paper peeled off before printing. This is a method of cutting stencils using this special commercial film, adhering the film to the silk screen and printing through the cut protections, suited where precise

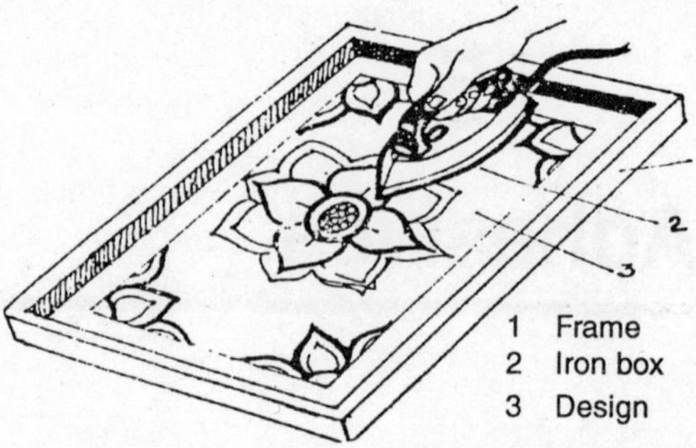

Transfer of shellac strencil once screen

and sharp edges are called for. After deciding the number of colours tape the film shiny side up, in place over the master drawing. Cut around the portions for the first colour, without affecting the backing paper. Register the cut film over the master drawing on the baseboard and make it adhere to the silk screen by few spots of glue, then by going through the inside with a pad saturated with adhering liquid followed by a dry pad. Now the film which has adhered may dry before peeling off the backing paper. Pin hole, leaks, *etc.,* are covered with two coats of lacquer. Printing is done from this stencil, screen cleaned, and film removed by any lacquer solvent. Subsequent colours are worked similarly.

Shellac knife-cut paper stencil

To prepare the thermo cement, remove wax melted on stove and adding 8 oz., rubbing varnish and one tablespoon corn starch, heat together. Melt down 1½ oz., beeswax. Lay good tracing paper over the master sketch and trace with pencil. Coat thick paper with the thermo varnish and let it set tacky in 30 minutes. Attach traced paper to support, coated paper. Apply a coat of 3½kg., cut shellac and let it set overnight. Cut and peel out same as with standard cutting films. Stretch and tack silk or organdy, in the usual way. Lay the screen directly down upon cut out shellaced paper and cutting support. Iron gently over sheet of paper with moderate heat. Turn screen over and strip away cutting support brought about by the heat action. Wipe face of stencil with cloth dampened in turps or naptha. Seal with shellac or clear lacquer and then tape.

Lacquer paper stencil

Make the master sketch, coat it with thermo-varnish cement. Coat the back of a good grade light weight tracing vellum with the same cement and place upon cement-coated master, stretch cement side down and roll together. Coat surface of vellum with two coats of good spraying lacquer, preferably with a spray gun. Or if desired, trace directly from the master sketch on vellum and apply to a separate cement coated cardboard or heavy paper and then lacquer. Alternately, sketch directly upon any light weight paper and place down upon cement coated cutting support . After lacquer dries, peel off gently the cut-out portions. Now, stretch and tack a silk of Nos. 6 to 10 or organdy using no. 3 or 4 tack. Place black screen directly down upon lacquered cutout paper with absolute contact. Dip soft cloth in lacquer thinner, squeeze it and apply to the inside of the screen over the cut out paper. Let screen set-in near a heater, turn over and strip away cutting support. With a cloth damped in Naptha or mineral spirit remove any cement left over.

Duplex decal (lacquer coated knife-cut) **stencil**

Standard size (25" x 36") duplex decalcomania paper consists of a thin vellum sheet gum coated and a heavy backing sheet fastened together, which can strip apart. Cut a piece of decal paper slightly larger than the master sketch. With the gum side up fasten down and spray twice clear spraying lacquer. Make the paper translucent by a coat of paraffin, oil with soft cloth. Fasten down to master sketch lacquer side up and peel portions for the openings as with cutting films. Eliminating oiling and the lacquer being applied afterwards, the sketch may be made directly upon the decal paper. In either way after stencil has been cut, place screen down in position on cut decal paper and place weight on frame. Dip a cloth in lacquer thinner, squeeze and wipe gently inside the screen over stencil, wipe with dry cloth and press. Turn screen over and strip away backing paper. Seal with clear lacquer in places left open between paper and frame.

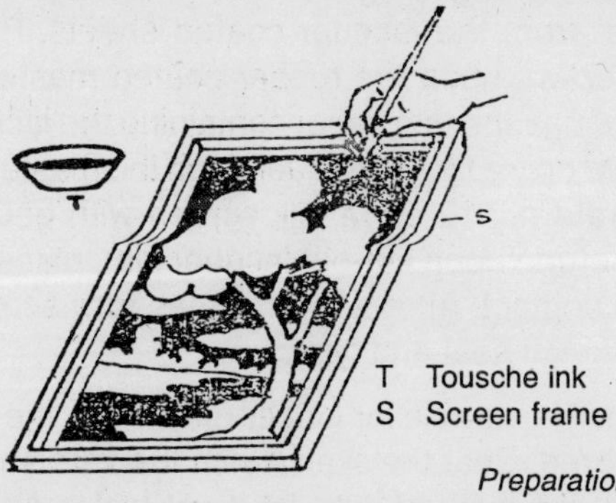

Preparation of stencil by tousche method

Duplex decal (shellac-coated knife-cut) **stencil**

Cut decal paper slightly larger than the sketch. Apply two coats of white shellac upon the gum coated side. After shellac is dry, turn over and oil the back with white spinole oil, turn wipe off with dry cloth making the paper translucent. Place the treated paper upon master sketch shellaced side up and tack down with thumb. Peel out open portions. Eliminating later oiling, sketch can be made directly upon the paper and shellac. After the stencil has been cut, place the screen in position down upon it. Iron in side of the screen with warm iron using newsprints between. Strip away the backing sheet. The vellum may now be removed by sponging. Only a thin shellac film is now left. After through sponging, the thin vellum release easily. Fill-in the open space between film and frame with shellac or lacquer. Clear with acetone or varnish remover for removing film from screen for reuse.

Duplex decal (glue-coat knife cut) **stencil**

This is printing with lacquer, acetate or oil base process colours.

Any good quality glue and gelatin may be used for brush coating, mixed with one ounce of the decal glue for ease in cutting film. Squeegee two cots of glue upon several sheets of duplex paper over gun-treated surface. Whether screen or brush coated oil back as in other decal paper methods. Now place a sheet of the treated paper glue side up, upon the master sketch. Cut the thin coated vellum film and peel off. Place black screen upon cut stencil in desired location. Dampen a piece of cardboard with water, and place it dampened side down inside the screen and iron. After ironing,turn screen over and strip away backing paper, seal and type.

Lacquer-film transfer stencil

Mix 1/4 oz., blue or orange spirit soluable aniline dye into one quart of clear spraying lacquer. Fasten down decal paper to flat support gummed side up and spray coloured lacquer. Spray a second coat after the first is dry. Paint the master sketch with a good grade of rubber frisket cement. Separate the backing sheet from the lacquer coated sheets. Place the lacquer coated sheet face down, upon the rubber coated master sketch and roll with rubber roller. Sponge the thin paper containing the lacquer film underneath, with water. Leave only a film of lacquer upon the master sketch. Peel out cut portions. Saturate no. 12 or 14 silk screen with good grade lacquer thinner, and place screen upon cut-out lacquer film, place a piece of paper inside and roll into contact. After a few minutes turn screen over and strip away the master sketch seal and type.

Celluloid knife-cut stencil is durable for longer runs. First, the drawing or lead pencil layout is prepared. Coat the sketch with the varnish cement mentioned in the shellac-stencil method, and let it set tacky. Apply .003 clear nitro cellulose celluloid with a rubber roller. Peel out cut portions as with other varieties of films. Sketch and tack no. 3 or 5 bolting silk or organdy upon the frame. Make a celluloid cement with equal proportion of C.P. acetone and amyl acetate. Over a wooden block 5 × 3 × 1-1/2 inches tack 2 folds of felt and four folds of coarse silk and trim excess. Place blank screen down upon celluloid stencil and sketch. Saturate pad with liquid cement and press out excess. Go over inside the screen, adhering celluloid. When thoroughly set, turn screen face up and detach sketch leaving the celluloid adhered to the screen. Paint the edges with liquid cement and press. Remove any varnish cement left on celluloid in removing master sketch with turps. In another variety the stencil sheet is formed of two layers, one being the stencil film and the other the backing paper adhering. After the stencil is prepared it is ironed to the screen base and backing sheet peeled off. Methylated spirit will wash the screen after use.

Blocked-out stencils (hand filled lacquer-glue)

Prepare full size master sketch. Tack no. 16 silk to the frame. Place screen down on master sketch and trace with pencil. In filling in use an illuminated frosted glass-top table. The filling in solution may be blue or black spraying lacquer or liquid glue added with show card white for body, water and glycerine. Tape inside of the screen with scotch tape. Seal the tape with glue or lacquer. Set screen upto register and process. After printing, the screen is cleaned, the filler being removed using lacquer solvent for lacquer, and water for glue. Clean twice and wipe dry. Repeat this for subsequent colours.

Key–line stencil process

Make master sketch in full size and colours. Place a no. 14/16 silk screen upon the sketch and trace with black waterproof drawing ink. Cut in using blocking lacquer, the opening for printing darkest colour of the sketch, *say* dark blue. Set screen up to register with master sketch "pin hinges" this method requiring absolute register use pegs of blocks for rigidity. Paint in upon the screen the portions which will remain in dark colour. Fasten screen to printing base with hinge pins and print second colour, *viz.,* medium blue. Block out portions of medium blue. Set screen up and print the third colour, *viz.,* light blue and then block out light blue portions. After printing the final colour or white the finished print should be an exact reproduction of the original master sketch. By this method unlimited number of colours can be laid.

For another similar method make the master sketch in full size, *for example,* one in four colours, blue, green, yellow and red on white card. Lay no. 14/16 silk screen upon the sketch and trace in with pencil or pen. Paint divisional lines and outside area with liquid glue. Paint first colour, *for example* blue and block out those portions with glue. This will also remain permanently in the screen. Now block out with lacquer every place except where green is to print. After printing and clean-up wash screen inside and wash out with lacquer-solvent. This does not affect the glue. Block out with lacquer everything excepting yellow, using key lines as guide. Similarly, proceed for all colours. To reclaim the screen, wash out with lacquer solvent and then with water.

Wash out screen (glue) **stencils**

First make pencil sketch or letter a show card. Sketch and tack no. 14/16 silk upon frame. Materials needed handly are liquid litho tusche, 12 ply cardboard, and squeegee, liquid glue, red sable, show card brush, *etc.* Trace in sketch on silk with lead pencil or pen. Now paint in tusche as lettering a design with another coat. Glue solution is prepared with ½ oz. glycerine, 6 oz., of liquid glue and 6 oz., of water. Pour a small quantity of the glue solution in one end of the screen and spread it over, around the design. After printing wash out tousche with naptha and glue with water. Instead of using glue preparation, lithograph crayons can be used. In colour works first print darkest colour and then superimpose transparent tones over the key print.

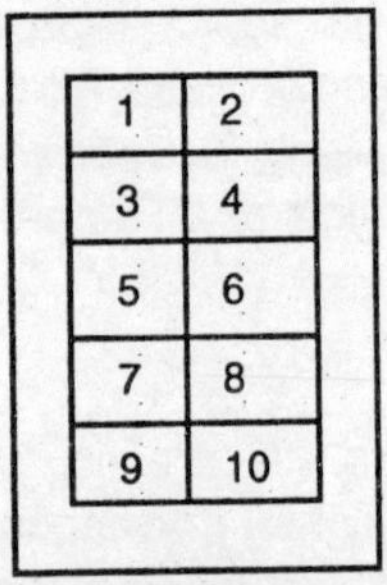

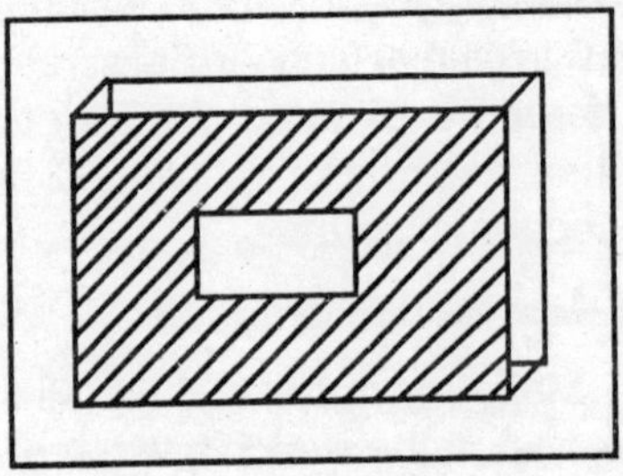

Polyvinyl alchohol photo process

To 12 oz., of ice water add 1 oz., of polyvinyl alchohol powder by sifting through a coarse silk pounce bag, stirring constantly. Heat the strained solutions to boiling point in a double boiler adding ¼ oz., granular bichromate of possasium. Water soluble dye may also be added for colour. Strain again and allow solution settle overnight. At-room temperature the cold sensitised solution is flowed to the face side of the screen. Squeegee down with a piece of cardboard and dry with a fan in the dark room. On a contact printing frame place positive and screen–lock-bars-felted block sensitized screen positive. Expose 18 to 20 minutes at 35 inches distance with 25 amp., are lamps or 15 minutes to direct sunlight. Remove exposed screen from printing frame and hose with hot water to develop and chill in cold water. To make the completed screen water resistant bake-in for 15 minutes. After drying in infra-red lamp or hardening with formaldehyde solution, the screen may be processed further for printing.

Numeral stencil (for right and left printing)

Make full size master sketch in one or more colours. Allow atleast ¼" bleed. After both sides of the cards are printed they may be trimmed or cut out. After master sketch is made, trace upon no. 14 or 16 silk with ink.

Using the key line lacquer block out, glue wash-out or direct photographic method proceed with making the screen stencil. After the masking medium has been applied attach another identical sandwiching the silk in between. Set the double frame screen to the printing base, fastening male sections of the pin hinges to both frames and in perfect alignment with the female section fastened to the base. Fasten another base upon regular base of the same thickness of a single frame and to fit inside the lower frame. Then adjust master sketch to design on the screen. Set register guides. Line with tape and seal. Print in one or more colours as required. To print all cards on the reverse side, simply turn screen over and fit into base hinge, tape and print.

Numeral stencil (Interchangeble)

First make the numeral sketch. Then cut stencil using film, cut paper, etc. Apply to no. 8 silk screen in the usual way. Lay the completed screen face down upon a piece of carboard and separate by cutting. Make another screen using no. 8 silk or organdy with an opening using cut film or hand filled.

Select the numeral cut screen stencils desired upon screen with opening using masking tape overlapping in edges. This forms a duplex type of stencil screen and we print in fact through two pieces of silk. Now for a quick change of one or more numerals simply remove the ones to be replaced by other without cleaning any part of the screen. These numerals can be cleaned and put away for future use. The above process may also be accomplished by first making the master sketch. Place the cutting film over it, cut and peel out. Then cut apart as per lines on sketch. Make ten small individual frames or a double set if needed. Wood ends and 1/8" thick by 1" wide steel sides, counter sunk holes and flat head screw Tack silk to the wooden ends, then stretch and glue with hot glue to the metal sides. Apply the cut film stencil in the usual way and seal. Make another frame so that the small screens will fit closely lengthwise. The top of wedge is for tightening or loosening with tap hamper.

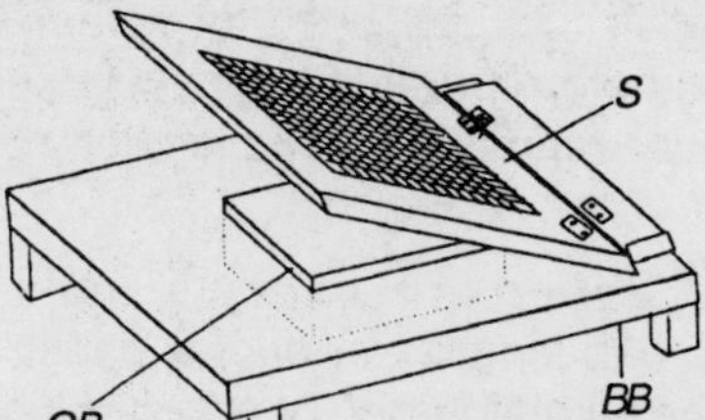

Screen printing on box
CB Carboard box B Base board S Screen

Now insert the small frames containing the numerals desired and lock up using the double wedge at one end, similar to printer's chase. Now the numerals can be screened all at one time with a divided blade squeegee or with a single one.

Different stocks in which screen printing can be done one paper-mat with and decorative finished, towards-pulp, ivory card, duplex and art boards.

Materials on which screen printing can be done

Both thermosetting and thermoplastic substances generally non-porus, non-absorbent and smooth can be screen printed. Ink for printing on plastic should be pre-tested for adhesion, water and humidity resistance stretch, acid, salt and weather resistance. Inks used for printing on thermosetting substrates are alkyd enamels, epoxy inks adhere to plastics by mechanical bond, dried by oxidation or polymerisation while lacquer inks are used on thermoplastics *like* acrylics, PVC, polyvinyl butyrate, cellulose acetate/butyrate, ethyl and nitro cellulose plastics.

Metallic foils are used in displays, name plates on aluminium foil 12 to 34 gauge and instrument dials. Metals of 12 (thinner) - 34 (thicker) SWG sheet is cleaned, washed with diluted acid to remove grease, coated with a primer, painted enamel white if necessary, cut to size and printed. After printing they are varnished for making scratch-proof. Oil based inks, matt or glossy, are used for printing on metal foil made of cellulose acetate, polyester and polystyrene bases are used for stickers, wall hangers and embossed effect, printed either single sheet or on roll.

Plastics Thermoplastic materials *like* acetal, acrylic, polypropylene, polyethylene, polybutylene, polycarbonate, poly propylene, acrylonitriles, butadiene, styrene, polyvinyl chloride, *etc.*, thermosetting materials-alkyd, metamine, phenolic, amino, epoxy, polyester, urea, urethane, cellulose acetate, ethyl cellulose and nitrate, etc.

PCBs are screen printed an copper-lad phenotics with acid-resistant inks, etched in acid epoxy resin, vinyl inks used on vinyl products, enamel and fluorescrent inks used for appropriate effect.

Ceramics are used for floor/wall decoration, kitchen and toiletry applications. Epoxy resin inks are used for screen printing on ceramics, dry varnish coat given before printing, product baked after printing. Glass is used for windows, car windshields and kitchenware, pre-heated before printing.

Decalcomania paper are used in making screen-process decalcomanias either with simplex or duplex paper. The former is coated directly on their surface with albumen or water-soluable gums. The duplex paper has a heavy backing sheet to which is adhered a removable tissue upon which the albumen or water-soluable gums are placed. Atmospheric conditions play a great deal with successful screen printing of decals.

16

Screen Printing on Glass

Colour medium for printing on glass are lacquer pastes, long and semi-long oil colours, printing inks in lakes and opaques, metallic oxide colours and short oil colours coated with varnish over the finished work. Screen process water colours can be used for temporary announcements or window display. Finer grades of silk are necessary for printing on glass surface, clean. Processing gold and silver leaf on glass is done by thin oiled stencil paper perforated for a pounce pattern. The design is pounced with dry red glass to be gilded. The glass is sized in easel and gilded similar to gilding a window sign. The gilded glass is placed gilded side up against the register guides on the printing table and the gilded design is backed up with the screen in either ling or semi long oil colour. After this backing colour is hard dry and after the excess leaf is removed, the shading outlining frosting, or whatever effect is desired is then printed by screen process. The mirror indoor flashing electric sign is made by first coating the glass with the mirror solution, transparent when held before a strong light. This is sprayed with clear lacquer which protects the delicate backing while the design is screen printed backward in transparent printing inks and opaques upon the lacquer mirrored background. The mirror slide is then placed in a frame front of a metal box which contains a flasher socket and lamp. When the lamp flashes off its reflection is seen luminous tubing effects *such as* those seen in cheaper indoor glass-faced electric signs are also obtainable by screen process. Imitation neon effect is obtained by processing solid black on the back of the glass leaving the design open. The design is then screen printed in the desired colour with transparent inks, or can be sprayed with the inks reduced to spraying consistency. To produce imitation neon effects on sprayed glass signs by the screen process method, a knife-cut shellac-adhered screen plate is used. The lettering or design is left open on the glass, and the open portions are sprayed with transparent lake printing inks thinned with spirit solvent.

Types of Photographic Stencils

1. Direct method in which the silk is coated with a sensitised emulsion, exposed to light and developed resulting in a stencil directly on the mesh of the silk-used for textile screening leaving a thin deposit of colour on the material screened.

2. A special pigment paper carbon tissue which forms the basic material and which is applied to the silk after processing, is used for jobs requiring clear-cut egest and fine detail. The carbon tissue may be made from a good 40 kgs., kraft or enamel paper is laid on a smooth surface and wiped with damp cloth. A cut piece of chocolate flexible gelatin is placed over the paper and rolled down with a roller which adheres to the damp surface. When the paper is dry, it is stored in metal tubes for future use. This paper is sensitised, exposed, developed and transferred to the screen. To make the paper waterproof, dip it in a solution made of 5 oz., of white shellac chips, 1 oz., of borax and one pint of water. The shellac chips and borax are digested nearly at boiling point until they are dissolved and the mixture is strained. After dipping in this solution the paper is hung up to dry. For making photographic stencils, perfect contact between negative or positive and the sensitised material when exposed through the printing frame or contact box is essential. Various types of lamps *like* 'photoflood' carbon and high pressure mercury vapour lamps give out intense light and are suited for exposure. The light sources should evenly distribute light while exposing. The distance between contact box and the light source may by: diagonal measurement of the job plus one third, and not nearer. Pigment paper is a film of gelatin with a backing paper sensitised and exposed to light along with the positive or negative rendering exposed portions insoluble. When pigment paper is developed in hot water the unexposed portions are washed away forming a stencil which is transferred to the silk frame. It is essential that positive should be opaque in image on a clear translucent background. The semi-transparent materials which can be used are various kind of tracing papers, tracing cloth, *etc.*, while the clear materials can be celluloid and plastic. The image can be reproduced through process plates or film. Images is traced on to the tracing paper or celluloid and painted in with opaque. Positive is used for making photographic stencils whereas negative will give a reverse effect. A camera can play an useful part in the process. Having the required positive and negative we could make three types of stencils from the two types of carbon tissue stencil papers *viz.*, autotype photo stencil paper no. 104, fast, and 1045. We shall now see the dry and wet methods under carbon tissue process.

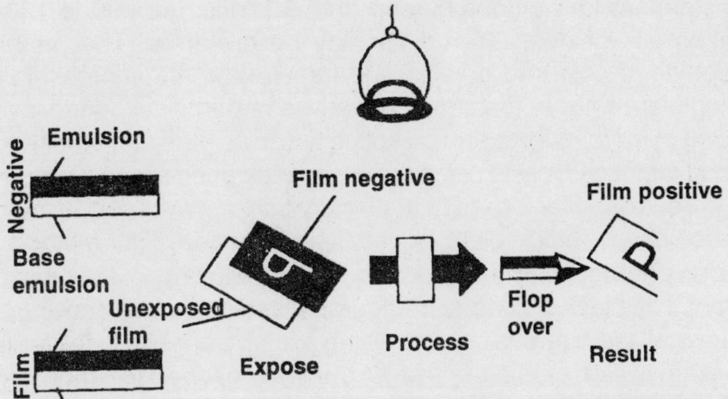

Making film positive from negative

5 Star film–exposure & development

Halftone screen and colour separation

With the colour originals, the net step is the preparation of negative and positive the latter emulsion side up. To reproduce the continuous tones of the original it is essential that a halftone screen with geometric formation or series of opaque parallel lines crossing both ways at right angles be used directly in front of the lens of the camera permitting the light rays enter through the minute transparent opening to the sensitised film. Various optical effects by manipulating the diaphragm and the focal length and many novel effects by using a fine copper wire screen instead of the regular halftone screen also be obtained. Good taffeta weave silk can be relied upon as standard for halftone screen upto 90 lines, from 90 to 120 lines finer bolting silk of nos. 20 and 25 may be preferred. The method of photographing of coloured objects and transferring the impression on to the printing plate without the use of negatives or prints has found favour in reproducing of merchandise and objecting which no perspective is required. The second method involves using three separate photographic plates each of which is sensitised for a particular primary colour. When plates are made for these colours a black plate is necessarily added. This method uses regular dry photographic film, developing in with hypo and making it transparent. The black and white photograph fastened to the drawing board with a piece of the film over it, and using transparent dyes, the yellow is applied with a red sable on the film in the proper location for the superimposing carry the red and blue, giving us the secondary colours in the designated sections. After applying yellow it is left interact on the photograph, and the film for red is attached and colour applied in the portions where red and orange are desired, not overlooking the portions of the original that will carry blue film is superimposed over the first two primary colours. From these coloured film halftone positive are prepared, using the actual photograph for the fourth colour or key plate which is printed first, and upon which the three primary transparent colours are superimposed. Other method is to prepare the original by hand life like as possible in flat poster technique in several grey tones from highlights to shadows. From this a straight halftone positive is made *like* Benday tinting effect. A set of four stencil screen plates are made from this positive, spotting out certain portions on each screen for the superimposing of the three primary transparent colours in printing using the fourth stencil for an added colour, if necessary. To determine the difference between negative and positive as applied to stencil screen process, one may bear in mind that a stencil screen plate prepared from a negative will require white or light tone printing on a dark coloured background while a stencil plate prepared from positive requires a white or light coloured background using dark colour inks fro printing. Methods of producing illustrations include photographic reproduction embracing halftone work, line drawings, and wood-cut effects, the super-imposing of transparent colours as well as coming screen plates for different effects.

Dry Method

To prepare sensitising solution, dissolve 3 ozs., granulate bicromate of potassium in a gallon of warm water in an enamel pan. For drying support clean a large polished sheet of tin plate, stainless steel or chromium plated ferrotype plate, with whiting and water. Chill solution to 60°C and strain. To sensitise the tissue, cut a piece of carbon tissue an inch smaller than drying support and submerge emulsion side up until it flattens out. Remove from sensitising both and squeeze, emulsion side down upon the plate, and dry. After paper is dry and before it release, strip from plate between two blotters underneath plate glass to prevent curling. For a temporary support clean a sheet 1/16" thick white vinylite with whiting and water-if stainless steel or polished brass is used, they need waxing. Tissue to be emulsion side down and positive emulsion side right side up. Cut a piece of tissue from the large pre-sensitised sheet, place emulsion side in contact with positive reading right side up. Expose for 15 minutes at 30 inches with no. 2 photoflood or 15 minutes at 40 inches with single or double are lamp. Remove exposed tissue from printing frame and submerge in cold water for two minutes, squeegee side down to the temporary support. Place support with tissue attached in hot water of 100°F, for a few minutes and strip off backing paper. Develop image by rocking and chill in cold water. Removing support and tissue from cold water, place them on flat surface, lower the screen inside and dry with fan. After the tissue dries, it adheres to the screen which is lifted, starting at one end of the film becoming transferred to the screen from the temporary support.

Wet Method : Prepare sensitizing solution as for the dry method and chill it. Cut a piece of 0.003 clear acetate an inch larger than the size of tissue and polish it using ferrotype wax solution, for a temporary support. Submerge cut tissue emulsion side up in the bath till it flattens out. Place tissue emulsion side down and squeegee to waxed temporary support. Place support with tissue between blotters to absorb excess solution. To make ready on printing frame, place glass or film positive emulsion side to read right side up and place support face down in contact with positive so that paper backing side of tissue is up. Then lock up. Exposure for wet tissue needs more time. A means to prevents tissue melting during exposure is an ice box. After exposure, remove tissue with support from printing frame. Fasten to the temporary support a metal plate or to a heavy sheet of white vinylite with marking type. Placing support in warm water, peel away backing paper. Develop out by agitating and chill in cold water. Place clear support on smooth surface image up and screen both gently. Place weight and fan dry. When tissue is dry, strip of transparent support, seal and tape;

For reverse effect, *i.e.*, background solid lettering in white, negative has to be made on a process camera and contact positive prepared in a contact printing frame using blue sensitive film. Orthochromatic film, sensitive to green, yellow, blue, violet and ultraviolet do not react to red, can be handled under red light in processing, used in process photographic work.

Panchromatic film sensitive to all colours are processed in dark, used for colour separation work.

Exposure distance varies on nature of original, light intensity and climatic conditions.

Sunlight is cheaper and better, in 150w bulb at a distance of 1½ foot exposure may take 3 hours, under 6 mercury vapour tubes at 1½ foot 15 minutes, which has to be settled by experience.

By using Novarace DTP butter paper good Xerox copier, direct positives can be had for cheaper screen printing, while film positive are desirable for quality work.

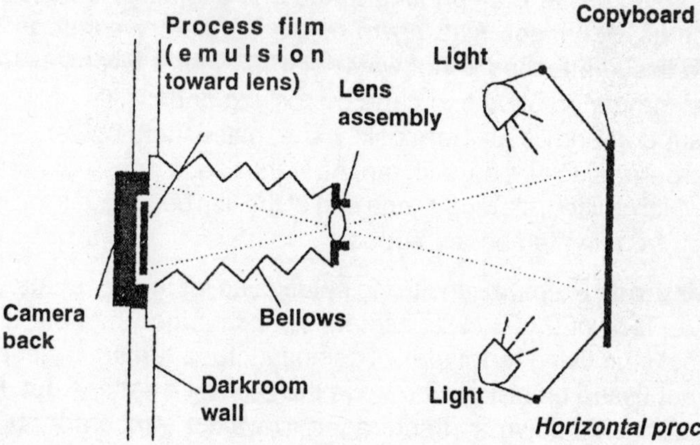

Horizontal process camera

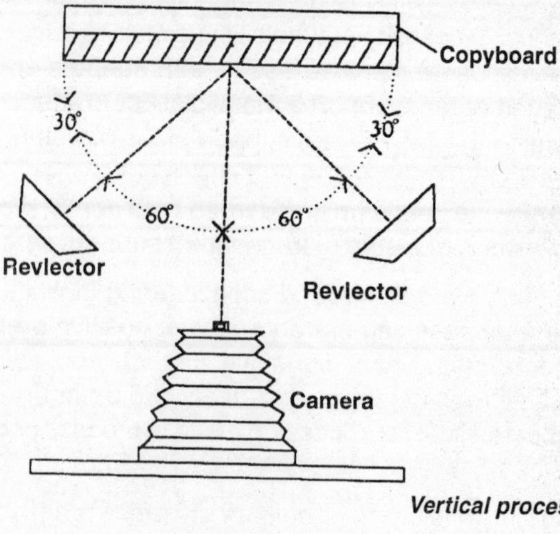

Vertical process camera

Moire Pattern

The best pictorial subjects are those free from solid dark masses and with soft gradation of highlights and shadows. We are dealing here with two screen patterns, one being the halftone screen and the other the mesh of the screen. When one is superimposed a moire interference results, which is avoided in two ways. The first method pre-imposes the silk of the screen and the halftone positive on a opaque table and moire effect avoided position marked on them as registration marks. The other method is by changing avoid moire, no. 16 silk being suitable for halftone work. The colour for halftone screen must not clog. The best medium is crystal base made with ethyl cellulose; poster colours with litho varnish also work well. Screen process enamel colours suit only coarse dots. Pure para rubber squeegee is better for this work.

Textile Printing

Screen printing on textile and wall paper is done by either individual sheets fed into a stationary or moving belt or printing in rolls on 60-80 metre long tables.

Textile printing inks consist of pigment and binder mixed in correct proportion with fixing agents for desired effect, light fast and resistance to washing detergents. On printing, curing is done from 5 minutes at 260°F and 1 minutes at 375°F or under sunlight for 15-20 minutes, depending on the fabric under printing. For printing on textile, 120 to 200 count mesh is used, printing base being felt, sponge, rubber or cotton pading, for flexible material a smooth, hard base being used. Pressure-sensitive wax table holding the cloth in register each piece of material having it's pulpboard lining. Stencil is held by short end placed on the cloth by contact stops and print is taken by drawing the squeegee to and fro, screen lifted and another print made. When entire length is completed, alternate gaps are printed. After colours are printed, cloth is untacked, steamed and finished, put through continuous washing, hot box for drying, calendered and ironed.

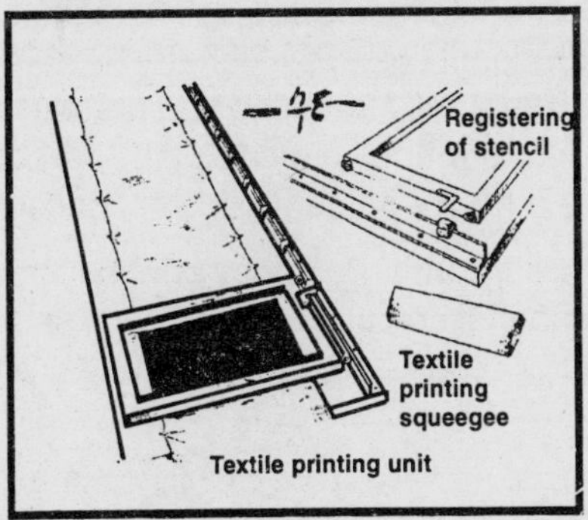

Textile printing unit

Until now four colour printing has had limited application to screen printing, inherent limitation being reproducing fine superimposed halftone dots, the concentration of which determines the density of the colour. Since only a solid colour is laid down in screen printing shading is accomplished by alternating dots of solid colour and white space which blends together at normal viewing distance are very small, and the finer the detail to be reproduced and the closer the viewing distance of the art the smaller the dot must be to carry the information, and this causes problems for the screen printer who until now has only coarse halftone screen of 65 or less dots per inch were only handled.

UV curing doubled the feasible line count that can be printed by screen process both by eliminating the drying problems in the screen and by making possible the use of coarse meshes to point the same halftone dot. UV process requires fine tuning involving a larger number of variables, including number of lamps, belt speed, squeegee thickness, pigmentation of ink, ambient temperature, *etc.* In making a screen, all four screens have to be exactly the same, in tune with the separations. If a screen is exposed differently a little heavier or a little lighter than another we are not reproducing what the separation were made for.

UV being predictable, we being to work with tools that the screen printer is not familiar *such as* the densitometer capable of measuring in minute detail the amount of light going through or being reflected off a piece of material, an *example* of the four colour application of this tool is the need in UV four colour curing for crucial control over film thickness, with a densitometer we can measure the difference between one print and another print accurately; tensometer, when working with four screen that must be stretched.

Screen printing is towards technological advacement and mechanisation *like* rotary printing machine for textile printing. Solvent–based having pollution problems, ultraviolet curing for instant drying of inks is developed, besides fluorescent colours which dry by dryers. Improvements in fabric meshes, stencil material, stretching and presses have taken place. Multicolour quarter tone printing involving not-so-complicated super imposition, has become a reality on ceramic tiles, balloons and T shirts.

For multicolour screen printing, latest printing machine consists of printing four or more number of colours, in continuous sequence and printed material either removed or drops on a conveyor under a drying system.

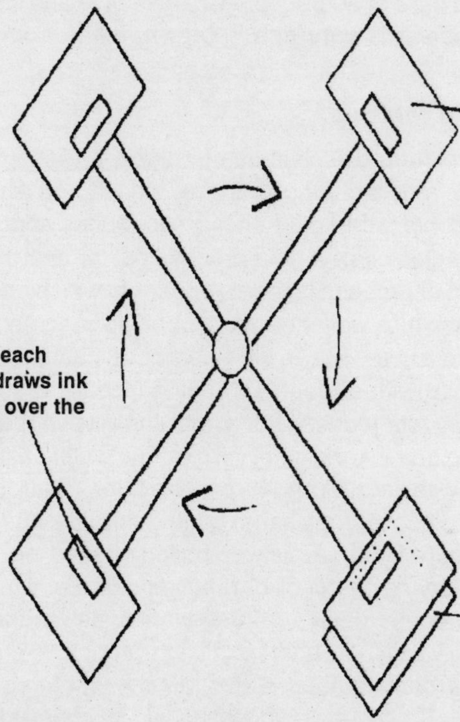

Process colours

Oil colour in paste form is commonly used in screening obtainable to dry with a gloss finish. Water colours suitably prepared work well. Pigments are ground in glycerine, gum-water, glucose molasses or honey being added for retarding. Titanium and zinc oxides may not be used in process colours for technical reasons, while lead can be used subject to its discolouring later. Carbon spectre in grades in used in process blacks. Lemon chrome yellow darkness at a heat of 250°F. Chrome yellow medium and chrome orange are fast to light, oil and water, darkness at 250°F. Fire red toner is also fast to light, water and alkali. Madder alizarin lake is fast to light, water oil and alcohol and heat fast upto 250°F. Toluidine toner and maroon are also fast to light, oil and water. Magenta is strong and bright. Permanent peacock blue is greenish, made with setoglancine on alumina hydrate, fast to light. Chinese blue is composed of ferric ferrocynide. Ultramarine blue is complex in compound consisting of aluminium, sodium, silica and sulphur. Purple toner is composed of methyl violet precipitated with phosphotungstic acid, strong toner colour and easy to grind. Emerald green is a mixture of 4 per cent Chinese blue and C.P. lemon yellow precipitated together. Chrome green medium is a mixture of 20 per cent Chinese blue and chrome yellow precipitated. Burnt sienna is very rich in brown, made from calcine raw siennz.

Colour Mediums and Vehicles

For air brush colours, dissolve water-soluble aniline colours in hot water with gum arabic mucilage or gelatine as binder, and alcohol-soluble aniline colours in alcohol with liquid shellac as binder and strain, more shellac improving the gloss. For a gold process paste, beat ¼, 1b. of gold lining bronze in ¼ pint of process lacquer reducer to which add a spoon of citric acid. Beat this mixture well into one pint of clear-screening lacquer, every time fresh before use. For a silver process paste, beat ½ 1b. of aluminum lining bronze with enough screening lacquer to make a paste and thin with screen lacquer reducer. For a gold and silver oil colour process pastes, mix gold lining bronze and lithol varnish into a stiff paste and thin to working consistency with varnish and turpentine drier. Retarding mediums for water colours are glucose, molasses, honey, certain kinds of glue, and glycerine; for oil colours-lithol varnish or boiled linseed oil; for lacquer-process colours-non-drying castor oil or rape seed oil. Paint free varnish is added to oil colour process pastes to prevent clogging in meshes-made with one quart of lithol varnish. ½ quart of mixing varnish, ¼ quart of oleum spirit, and ½ pint of turpentine Japan drier. Mix the first three by agitation before adding the drier. To make a gold writing ink, mix honey and gold leaf in equal parts to fine consistency. Agitate with 30 parts of hot water and allow the mixture to settle. Decant water and repeat washing several times. Finally dry the gold and mix it with weak gum arabic solution for use. Liquid gold for vellum is made by grinding gold leaf with gum water in a mortar and adding little bichloride of mercury.

Waterproofing vehicle – To make showcard colours and inks waterproof, add a strained solution made of 5 oz., of white shellac chips, one oz., borax, and one pint of water in which the shellac chips and borax are digested at nearly boiling point until dissolved.

17

Colour Combination

Here are colour combinations for popular colours.

Brass	:	32 parts zinc white, 6 parts cadmium yellow medium, 6 parts yellow ochre, 1 part raw umber.
Brick red	:	16 parts zinc white, 8 parts yellow ochre, 1 part venetian red, trace of burnt umber.
Bud green	:	8 parts zinc white, 3 parts cadmium lemon, 3 parts cobalt blue.
Carrot	:	64 parts zinc white, 10 parts cadmium orange, 1 part cadmium red light.
Chocolate brown	:	1 part zinc white, 1 part burnt umber, 1 part burnt sienna.
Flame	:	1 part zinc white, 1 part burnt orange.
Grape fruit	:	8 parts zinc white, 1 part cadmium lemon, trace of raw umber.
Khaki	:	8 parts zinc white, 3 parts yellow ochre, 1 part raw umber, traces of burnt umber, cobalt blue.
Ocean green	:	40 parts of zinc white, 1 part cadmium lemon, 1 part cobalt blue.
Pea green	:	10 parts zinc white, 1 part cadmium lemon, 1 part cobalt blue, trace of burnt umber.
Sandalwood	:	35 parts since white, 2 parts burnt umber, 1 part burnt sienna, trace of raw umber.
Sky blue	:	400 parts zinc white, 1 parts monastral blue, 1 part alizarin crimson.

Tobacco brown : 4 parts raw sienna, 2 parts zinc white, 1 part burnt umber.

Tomato : 8 part zinc white, 8 parts cadmium orange, 1 part cadmium red light, 1 part raw sienna.

Wild rose : 65 parts zinc white, 1 part alizarin crimson, trace of ultramarine blue.

Legibility from distance *(in order)*

Black on yellow, black on orange, yellow-orange on navy blue, bottle green on white, scarlet-red on white, black on white, navy blue on white, white on navy blue, yellow- orange on black, white on black, white on bottle green white on scarlet-red, white on purple, *etc.*

Among the five essentials in colour separation work for screen process printing it is important that the processor should have a thorough knowledge of the proper colours and their application, preparation of coloured sketch, selecting proper negative for use, selecting screen plates, and laying of the colours. To avoid mis-registration, the set of stencils should be exact, free from slightest degree of expansion or shrinkage, which can be accomplished with proper sensitiser and correct treatment of the cloth. An opaque colour should be used for the fist colour although transparent colours laid over white are brilliant than solid ones.

Drying racks are needed for drying finished jobs or multicoloured job between different workings racks may be vertical horizontal or at an angle. The wire screen rack which is used for decalcomania transfers are covered with fine wire screen preventing the decalcomanias from sagging and affording plenty of air circulation for drying. Upright racking is suitable for drying screen processed metal, wood or glass,. Individual racking method is placing one at a time on the truck, one above another after the preceding one is full with printed material. Prints may also be dired on ropes and with small wooden or plastic clips as illustrated below.

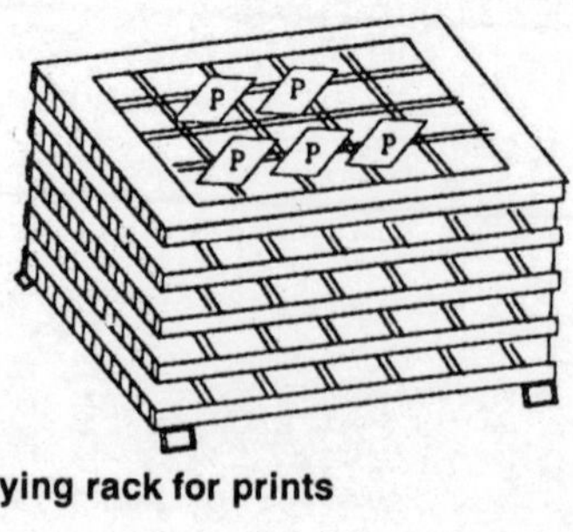

Drying rack for prints

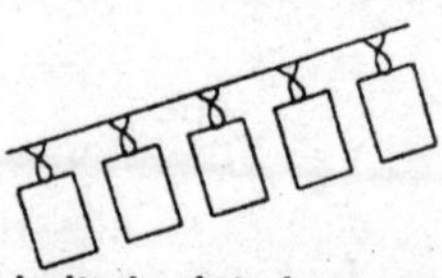

Limited prints hung on clips on a rop to dry under air circulation

Cellulose and lacquer inks dry in 15-30 minutes while oil based inks take few hours to dry. In the conventional drying systems drying of prints take place penetration or absorption on highly absorbent and open structured paper.

Oxidation as in cartons and less absorbant substrates, consuming. Solvent evaporation where energy requirement is large.

Due to the need of a drying system avoiding use of large quantities of organic solvents and which by some reaction dry or cure the print instantaneously UV and the electron beam radiations were introduced. UV curing ink cosists a coating of mixture with liquid prepolymers and monomers together with pigment and photo active compound. When a UV curing ink is printed and exposed to UV light source, the photoinitiater breaks up into free radicals, which initiate a polymerisation reaction which in turn cross-link the monomer to from a solid film. UV radiation curing equipment consists of UV source, reflectors and accessories. A common source UV used for the curing is an arc tube consisting of a quartz envelope filled to a medium pressure with mercury vapour, operating temperature of the lame being 700°C emitting energy wave lengths which are in resonance with the initiater. Reflectors are highly polished for maximum reflectivity.

Ancillaries for UV curing

Shuttering for power cut to protect the printed sheet when printing speed reduces.

Cooling : The temperature of the tube being 700°C, leads to over heating, lamps are cooled by drawing air their surface.

Instant drying is now possible to make UV inks which will cure in less than a second, therefore the prints can be handled at press and without loss of time. The gloss of the UV cured print is good and compares favourably with that obtained with conventional quick setting inks.

The rub resistance of the UV cured print is excellent and it is developed immediately the print is off the press. All these has opened up new avenues in the printing industry *like* the printing on non-absorbent substrates *like* foil, lined boards, metalised papers, polythene lined boards, *etc.*

However, the basic cost of UV curing inks is high, because the resins (prepolymers) are expensive than those that are used in conventional quick setting inks.

Infrared being a heating process, exposure of screen prints to infrared radiation accelerates penetration, evaporation and oxidation and drying. There is no cross linking of the components of the ink and there is no instantaneous drying like in UV systems. Infrared heating is far too economical compared to UV curing.

Market for screen printing is explorable by educating the clients, *i.e.*, individual professionals *like* accountants, consultants, practising lawyers, for their visiting cards and letterheads, shops selling items *like* footwear for window displays, *for instance* Bata showroom display are printed by silk screen process, small advertising agencies, political parties, computer training and educational institutes, vendors, sellers of domestic appliances, *etc.*, for banners *including* your fixing them up overnight, sticker users *like* computer assemblers, toy, accessories and furniture makers, watch, TV, etc., dial makers.

Like any other business, printing orders are to be sought by constant touch with customer touch with customers and giving them prompt service. Printing orders are sought by screen printer himself who knows the final effect of the design and colour matching, carries samples of work, able to quote on the spot, but his attention is divided between marketing, production and bill realisation, not being able to afford full-time salesmen. Salesmen trained in sales, through not necessarily in screen printing seek orders on behalf of printer or secure orders and have them printed. Being extroverts, they apply knowledge of selling, not concerned with working capital needs or labour problem, interested in their commission which is paid on realisation. Middlemen and advertising agencies, normally technically knowledgeable with typographical sense, able to advise the clients on design, choice of paper, cost, *etc.*, have contacts but gets printing done by printers-well or ill equipped-but, jobs getting delayed for the user clients and cost marked up. Delivery promises should be adhered to, besides excellent client servicing. A user list can be prepared, city-wise for marketing. Knowledge of estimating including price of paper and other raw materials is important for salesmen.

Developing countries in Asia and Africa, for growing soft drink market, have to print millions of bottles every week for which the principals *like* Pepsi or Coca-Cola could encourage setting up modern screen printing machines with dryers, on joint venture, which leading Indian screen printers may explore.

Project cost & Viability

	Scale	
	Small	*Tiney*
Capital (Rs.'000)		
Equipment & accessories	25	200
Working	15	50
Area required (sq. mtrs)	20	50
Monthly :		
Raw materials	5	25
Wages	5	15
Others	3	10
Likely value of work to be executed	25	75
Profitability	4	20

18

Silk Screen Photo Stencil Preparation

In the modern age of mechanization and automation, it is comforting to know that craftsmanship still reigns supreme in the field of silk screen. Nevertheless, a wise silk screen artist endeavours to make best use of the facilities which photography has extended to this process. In the past, the silk screen artist also used to be endowed with drawing and designing ability but that is not so at present. Thanks to photography, any design can be photographed and most of them can be reproduced by silk screen. The varsatility of the process is unquestionable since one can print on almost any surface paper, board, fabric, glass, bakelite, wood etc. and it is not even necessary that the substrate receiving the ink should be plane and flat.

Before preparing a photostencil, one must have a sharp positive of the design or original to be reproduced. Most of the silk screen reproduction consists of line work though halftone work also been attempted successfully.

The conventional method of making a photographic positive is by contacting a negative on a piece of process film. The negative is made on a process camera or any other camera suitable for copying work. The original design is placed on the copyboard of the camera and evenly illuminated by a suitable illuminate which may be carbon arc lamp or white light fluorescent tube or photoflood lamp to name a few. The camera lens must be good anastigmat. An apochromat lens would be ideal but quite expensive at the same time. Having focussed the original to the desired size, a sheet of orthochromatic line film or ortho lith film is loaded in the camera and exposure is given to the original. The orthochromatic film is not sensitive to red region of the spectrum (600-700 millimicrons;). Hence the film can be processed in a dark room fitted with red safelight. Development is done in the developer recommended by the film manufacturer. If the recommended developer is not available, any one of the following developers may be used.

1. Caustic – Hydroquinone developer

Solution 'A'

Hydroquinone	25 gm
Potassium metabisulphite	25 gm
Potassium bromide	25 gm
Water to make	1000 c. c.

Solution 'B'

Potassium hydroxide	50 gm
Water to make	1000 c. c.

For use, mix A and B in equal volume just before use. During development, the exposed areas of the film are affected and the silver halides present in these areas are converted into a form of black silver. Thus opacity is produced in the exposed areas. The developed film is then quickly washed in water in the following solution :

Sodium thiosulphate (hypo)	250 gm
Water to make	1000 c. c.

The above solution reacts chemically with the residual silver halides forming a water-soluble complex so that when the negative is washed, the soluble complex is removed from the gelatin layer.

2. Hydroquinone – Carbonate developer

Sodium Sulphite (anhydrous)	150 gm
Hydroquinone	20 gm
Sodium Carbonate (anhydrous)	50 gm
Potassium Bromide	10 gm
Water to make	2000 c. c.

The above is a single solution developer which must be used undiluted. Development time is five minutes at 20°C.

Whichever developer is used, if the negative is correctly made, the design will be obtained in a transparent form against an opaque background.

Preparation of positive

A positive is now made from the above negative by contact printing. The operation is performed in a printing cabinet of the vacuum type. If such a cabinet is not available, a photographic contact printing frame may be used. If that too is not available, two thick glass plates may be used. The emulsion side of the film is placed in contact with the emulsion side of the negative. The combination is held together between the two glass plates. Exposure is given through the negative using a frosted glass filament lamp. Lamp will be transmitted through the transparent areas of the negative (which constitute the image of the design) and expose the film. There after the film is processed as in making the negative. The result is an opaque against a transparent background.

Positive Making by Chemical Reversal

Instead of preparing negative a positive can be directly prepared by chemical reversal. In this method, the copy is exposed and the film is developed in the recommended developer. The exposure must be somewhat greater than normal and has to be determined by trial and error. After development, the negative is well washed in water. Then the silver formed in the exposed areas is removed by 'bleaching' in the following solution :

Solution A

Cupsic nitrate	300 gm
Potassium bromide	10 gm
Acetic acid	150 c.c.
Water to make	1000 c.c.

Solution B

Hydrogen peroxide	2 %

The working solution is prepared by mixing A and B in equal volumes. The solution dissolves the gelatin in the exposed areas. When 'bleaching' is complete, white light is switched on and the bleached negative is washed in water. The unexposed silver halides in the image areas are now exposed by the light. The film is then redeveloped, washed and fixed. The result is positive.

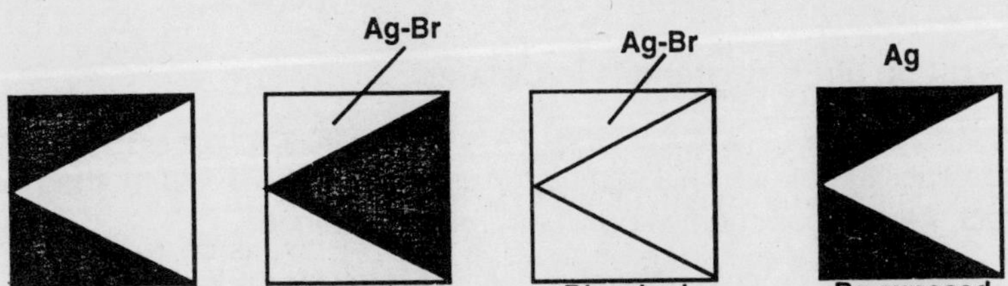

Original Design — **Negavtive before fixing** — **Bleached negative** — **Re-exposed redeveloped and fixed positive**

Colour Separation

Line colour separation, we more as many positive as the number of colours. These positive are prepared from akey negative of the original design which is drawn in black and white with an overlay sheet indicating the colours desired in different areas. The scheme of colour separation is as below.

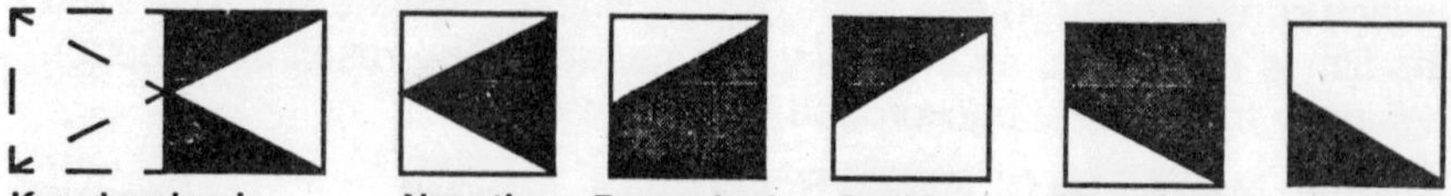

Key drawing in black & white with overlay sheet | **Negative** | **Retouched negative blue area stopped out** | **Positive for red colour** | **Retouched negative Red area stopped out** | **Positive for blue colour**

The original is a Flag in two colours-red and blue. A negative (ii) is made from the key drawing. The negative is retouched with photo-opaque leaving only the red areas open. A positive (iv) is made from this negative which will be used in making the red printing photostencil. The key negative is now washed and dried. It is again retouched (v) to stop out all areas except blue. Another positive (vi) is made from the negative which will yield the blue photostencil.

Halftone Reproduction by Silk Screen

Although it is possible to prepare photostencils for halftone reproduction, the result cannot be of a high quality. The limitations imposed by the process make it mandatory (i) to use a screen not finer than 33 lines per cm (85 lines per inch) and (ii) to avoid fine tonal gradation because it is neither possible to maintain fine isolated gelatin dots in the shadows nor force the ink through very fine openings in the highlights areas of the gelatin stencil. For best results, negative (halftone) must be made on a process camera using lith films or coarse magenta contact screens. The negative is contact printed on high contrast film to obtain positive with dense and sharp dots.

Preparation of Photostencils in Gelatin

The positive (line or halftone) so prepared is now used in obtaining a photostencil in gelatin. This can be done either by the direct method or by indirect method commonly known as transfer method.

In the direct process, a layer of gelatin of suitable thickness is deposited over the silk screen. A number of coating solutions have been recommended by different workers. The following is a typical formula which gives fairly good results :

Gelatin	90 gm
Sodium Carbonate	2 gm

Potassium bichromate	20 gm
Glycerine	7.5 c.c.
Water	1000 c.c.

Gelatin is the film forming colloid which is rendered light sensitive by potassium dichromate. Glycerine makes the stencil pliable so that it may not develop cracks. Sodium carbonate raises the pH of the solution by reducing its acidity. A dye such as methyl violet may also be added to impart colour and improve the visibility of the image in the stencil.

In preparing the solution, gelatin is first soaked in about 600 cc of water and then warmed to a temperature of about 45°C to obtain an emulsion. The dichromate and the carbonate are separately dissolved each in 200 cc of water. When the gelatin has dissolved the carbonate and bichromate solutions are added taking care that the temperature is maintained at 45°C. The glycerine and the dry are added last. The emulsion is thoroughly stirred.

For coating, the emulsion is warmed to 45 + C and applied to the screen by a wide camel's hair brush. Both sides of the screen are coated and care is taken to obtain a film of even thickness on the silk screen. Drying is effected by a fan. Both sides of the screen are then given a second coating. The coating and the drying operations must be carried out in yellow light otherwise the coating solution is likely to get fogged.

The sensitized screen is now printed under the positive. Actinic light should be used for exposure. Development is done in water at 40°C. Both sides of the stencil are developed until the unexposed gelatin has been washed away leaving a clear cut design in the stencil. Development is arrested by applying cold water. Linen sheets are then used to absorb as much moisture from the stencil as possible. Further drying of the stencil is done under a fan.

After printing, the gelatin stencil is soaked in twenty-percent solution of sodium or potassium hydroxide and then scrubbed under warm water all traces of gelatin have been removed.

The transfer process though somewhat expensive is extremely popular these days since it is quick working and gives excellent results if the manufacturers instructions are followed. A large variety of materials are obtainable based on transfer process of which two are being described below.

The first is a presensitized red pigmented gelatin coated on a transparent polyester of base of good dimensional stability. The product is commercially available as 'Five Star' and is manufactured by Autotype International Limited, England. The film can be handled in yellow light. Stencil preparation is extremely simple. The film is first cut to the desired size. The positive is placed in contact with the non-gelatin side so that the stencil will be right reading when viewed from the gelatin side of 'Five Star'. While maintaining a firm contact, exposure is given through the positive using a source of actinic light such as a carbon are lamp or mercury vapour lamp. Sunlight may also be used. The sensitivity of 'Five Star' lies mostly in the ultraviolet and blue region of the spectrum. Exposures vary a great deal since there are many variants. It is therefore best to find correct exposure by first making a trail exposure.

The next step after exposure is hardening of the exposed areas of gelatin. This is done by immersing the film in 1.2% solution of hydrogen peroxide at 20°C. The commercially available hydrogen peroxide has its strength expressed in 'Volumes'. Thus a 20 volume solution contains about 6% of hydrogen peroxide.

The gelatin film is then developed in a spray of warm water at 40-45°C until all the unexposed gelatin has been removed from the image area. The silk screen which has been previously cleaned is moistened with water and the stencil is applied to the underside of the frame carrying the screen. Moisture is removed by gently dabbing with clean newsprint which is placed inside the frame. Thereafter, the stencil is allowed to dry in gentle breeze of a fan. The base support is then peeled off.

In another indirect process, the film material is supplied unsensitized alongwith a liquid emulsion and a sensitizer. The emulsion and the sensitizer are first mixed and then coated on the unsensitized film through the silk screen. The coating is allowed to dry after which the backing material of the film is removed. Exposure through the positive is given as before so that the image will be right reading when viewed from the top side of the screen frame. Development is done in plain water. Finally, cool water (20-21°C) spray is directed over the surface until the image areas are washed away. The stencil is then dried as before.

Ten Golden Rules for Reconditioned Machines

And so it came to pass that many dealers of used graphic arts equipment practised their skills, spreading joy and goodness in the oversized pages of the most widely-read and most well-respected paper for graphic arts readers.

And lo, many of them spoke of their minds and their hearts to the classified ad manager of this publication, and they told him secrets of their experiences in dealings of the heavy iron; and he listened.

And in the fourth month of ninth year of the ninth decade of the twentieth century of the modern era, there was produced a very wonderful issue of this most-revered paper, and it was called the "Used Equipment Roundup".

Thus it was that the classified ad manager gathered to himself their notes and records of such secrets as he had collected over time from these wise and seasoned veterans of the trade.

And he sifted through them, and pored over them and digested them, and drank much of the bitter fruits in order to understand them the better, and meditated upon these pearls of wisdom at length.

And when he could stand no more, he distilled them into words, and his head swam with the richness of it, and he begat for all who would read of it.

1. Thou Shalt Buy Only From Reputable Source.

No rule on buying used equipment is more important than this one.

If you haven't had business dealings with the seller personally, ask for references. Any reputable dealer will be happy to supply you with a list satisfied customers.

If you buy through a private sale, you may think you're getting a really "hot deal". On the other hand, you may just get burned!

Any used equipment dealer will tell you: his reputation is his important asset. Take advantage of this fact and get the goods on your man before the goods go on your van.

2. Thou Shalt Plan For Thy Needs, Present and Future

The worst thing you can do is to buy equipment that is just sufficient to handle your present needs (unless you have no plans to grow).

If in six months you find your sales have outgrown you machinery, you'll be faced with taking a cash loss on the disposal of your present equipment and a loss in production time when you set up its replacement.

Plan carefully for the short term and the long term. Be sure the equipment you're getting today will be compatible with whatever you intend to add down the road.

3. Thou Shalt See a Machine Running Whenever Possible

Be prepared to travel, if necessary, to see equipment in operation. This, of course, goes in spades for major piece.

Don't take the seller's word for it that the machine runs "perfectly" or "just like new".

If you don't feel you have adequate knowledge with regard to the purchase, take along an expert to check the machine's performance. If you have to, pay a qualified independent serviceman or experienced operator-mechanic to go along with you when you make inspection.

Whatever you do, don't rely on a "friend who used to be in the business" or a brother-in-law who once worked for a printer, or the like.

4. Thou Shalt Not Buy Equipment Too Big For Your Shop

This is a perfectly obvious, straight-forward rule and one that is overlooked every day.

Before you buy, ask yourself: will this machine fit through my door? Up the stairs? Down the stairs?

If your shop is on the second floor, will you have to hoist it up the side of the building to get it in? Then what?

If you're in the basement, can you get it down there without having to dig a special tunnel for it?

Will the floor hold it safely?

Will you have to completely disassemble it? Who's going to pay for the expense of moving it if it turns out it won't go in?

If you don't manage to get it in, will there be enough room left to run it without continually hitting or falling over something?

Think ahead. It may save you a barrel of aggravation.

5. Thou Shalt Check Electrical Compatibility

Make sure your available power source is compatible with the machine you're buying.

Many paper cutters and larger presses require 550 volt or 220 volt three-phase power. If you don't have three-phase hydro in your building, you may have a problem. It may be very expensive to install it; it may even be impossible.

If your building does have three-phase hydro, you will still have to install a small transformer. This however, should not present a major difficulty.

Whatever you do, don't confuse 220 volts one-phase (domestic hydro) with 220 volts three-phase (industrial hydro).

6. Thou Shalt Ask For Details on "Reconditioning".

Remember that "reconditioned", "refurbished" and "rebuilt" are sometimes used interchangeably.

Find out exactly what has been done to the machine, and by whom. Ask a lot of questions. If answers aren't forthcoming, or seem vague or noncommittal, pass on the deal. Too often "recondition" machines are sold with nothing more elaborate than a fresh paint job.

Inspect your potential purchase inside and out before you make a commitment.

7. Thou Shalt Be Sure Parts And Service Are Readily Available.

Every machine, no matter how well it runs when you first get, is destined to need service and/or replacement parts sooner or later.

When it does, will you be able to find a reliable technician to work on it? If you do, will he be able to get the parts he needs without waiting weeks or months for them? If it is an obsolete model, parts may not be available at all.

Bargains can sometimes be had on machines with unfamiliar names – but beware if you need service.

If, like most people, you can't afford lengthy down time, stick to equipment made by manufacturers with established networks of service and parts suppliers. When it breaks down in the middle of your busiest time, you'll be glad you did.

8. Thou Shalt Cover Delivery, Installation And Operator Training.

If delivery and installation is not included in the price, you will have to pay movers, carpenters, electricians, etc., out of your pocket. Have you figured this into calculations?

In addition, if the equipment you are buying is unfamiliar and/or complicated is the seller going to provide any kind of training?

If not, you may find the true cost of the equipment is a great deal more than you anticipated after you add the extra time it will take for an operator to learn by himself how to run it properly and the productivity you lose in the process.

9. Thou Shalt Determine Trade-Back Options And Allowances.

"The best laid plans of mice and men", as they say, can go away.

What if, after all your careful consideration, the machine doesn't perform up to your expectations, or your needs change faster than you expected? Will the seller take back the machine? If so, on what terms?

This is an important point to establish. In the case of a private sale, you will have to dispose of the equipment yourself. Some dealers, however, offer "trade up" or "trade-back" programs with varying terms and conditions.

10. Thou Shalt Have A Warranty in Writing.

Whatever "guarantees" or "warrnaties" are included by the dealer, make sure you have them in writing.

There's nothing worse than going back sometime later with "I thought you said..."

At the same time, you should satisfy yourself that the seller is in a position to live up to his promise.

19

Plant Economics of Screen Printing on Cotton, Polyester & Acrylic

Rated Plant Capacity	=	500.00 Pcs/Day
LAND & BUILDING (Land Area 500 Sq.mts.)	=	Rs. 3,65,000.00

Plant & Machinery

1. Printing table
2. Screens
3. Gumming machine
4. Washing Machine
5. Guides, Squeezas, etc.
6. Miscellaneous

FIXED CAPITAL

1. LAND & BUILDING	Rs.	3,65,000.00
2. PLANT & MACHINERY	Rs.	1,97,000.00
3. OTHER FIXED ASSETS	Rs.	1,10,000.00
TOTAL	Rs.	6,72,000.00

Raw Materials

1. Pieces to be printed
2. Pigment, colour, dyes, etc.
3. Miscellaneous

TOTAL WORKING CAPITAL/MONTH

1.	RAW MATERIAL	Rs.	5,20,000.00
2.	SALARY & WAGES	Rs.	27,000.00
3.	UTILITIES & OVERHEADS	Rs.	34,750.00
	TOTAL	Rs.	5,81,750.00

TOTAL CAPITAL INVESTMENT

TOTAL FIXED CAPITAL	Rs.	6,72,000.00
TOTAL WORKING CAPITAL FOR 2 MONTHS	Rs.	11,63,500.00
TOTAL	Rs.	18,35,500.00

TURN OVER/ANNUM

By sale of 1,50,000 pieces	Rs.	93,00,000.00

PROFIT SALES RATIO = PROFIT / SALES X 100 = 21.67 %

RATE OF RETURN = OPERATING PROFIT / T.C.I X 100 = 109.81 %

BREAK EVEN POINT (B.E.P) = 22.94 %

20

Plant Economics of Heat Transfer Label By Screen Printing Process

Rated Plant Capacity	=	100000 Labels/Day
LAND & BUILDING (Land 150 sq. mts.)	=	Rs. 2,90,000.00

Plant & Machinery

1. Stainless Steel Tank (with Jacket) with agitator
2. Closed top S.S. tank
3. Screen Printing equipment system
4. Miscellaneous tools, jigs, fixtures etc.

FIXED CAPITAL

1. LAND & BUILDING	Rs.	2,90,000.00
2. PLANT & MACHINERY	Rs.	1,46,000.00
3. OTHER FIXED ASSETS	Rs.	1,15,000.00
TOTAL	Rs.	5,51,000.00

Raw Materials

1. Aniline Oil
2. Potassium chlorate
3. Distilled water
4. Hydrochloric Acid
5. Copper Chloride
6. Latex
7. Sulphur

8. M.B.T.
9. Yellow Pigment
10. Cellophane film
11. Packaging Materials

TOTAL WORKING CAPITAL/MONTH

1. RAW MATERIAL	Rs.	51,213.50
2. SALARY & WAGES	Rs.	16,800.00
3. UTILITIES & OVERHEADS	Rs.	13,000.00
TOTAL	Rs.	81,013.50

TOTAL CAPITAL INVESTMENT

TOTAL FIXED CAPITAL	Rs.	5,51,000.00
TOTAL WORKING CAPITAL FOR 3 MONTHS	Rs.	2,43,040.50
TOTAL	Rs.	7,94,040.50

TURN OVER/ANNUM

By sale of 300 Lakhs stickers for Rubber tyres	Rs.	30,00,000.00

PROFIT SALES RATIO = PROFIT / SALES X 100 = 60.98 %

RATE OF RETURN = OPERATING PROFIT / T.C.I X 100 = 230.40 %

BREAK EVEN POINT (B.E.P) = 15.73 %

21

Plant Economics of Cloth Printing

Rated Plant Capacity	=	5000 Mtr/Day
LAND & BUILDING (Land Area 1000 sq.mtr)	=	Rs. 7,50,000.00

Plant & Machinery

1. Printing screens withh various designs
2. Printing tables
3. Dye mixing machine
4. Washing & Treatments tanks (R.C.C. work)
5. Baby boiler
6. Mangles and rollers
7. Drying machine continuous conveyor type
8. Motors and other mis/units like mangles etc.
9. Exposure cabinate
10. Screen stretcher
11. Squeeges
12. Miscellaneous

FIXED CAPITAL

1. LAND & BUILDING		Rs.	7,50,000.00
2. PLANT & MACHINERY		Rs.	6,05,000.00
3. OTHER FIXED ASSETS		Rs.	85,000.00
	TOTAL	Rs.	14,40,000.00

Raw Materials

1. Chemicals, Dyes etc.

TOTAL WORKING CAPITAL/MONTH

1. RAW MATERIAL	Rs.	6,25,000.00
2. SALARY & WAGES	Rs.	64,875.00
3. UTILITIES & OVERHEADS	Rs.	32,750.00
TOTAL	Rs.	7,22,625.00

TOTAL CAPITAL INVESTMENT

TOTAL FIXED CAPITAL	Rs.	14,40,000.00
TOTAL WORKING CAPITAL FOR 3 MONTHS	Rs.	21,67,875.00
TOTAL	Rs.	36,07,875.00

By screning printing 1500000 meters Rs. 1,20,00,000.00

PROFIT SALES RATIO = PROFIT / SALES X 100 = 19.52 %

RATE OF RETURN = OPERATING PROFIT / T.C.I X 100 = 64.93 %

BREAK EVEN POINT (B.E.P) = 38.30 %

22

Plant Economics of Screen Printing

Rated Plant Capacity = 40000 Nos/Day

LAND & BUILDING (Land Area 200 sq.) = Rs. 1,51,000.00

Plant & Machinery

1. Auto Flat Screen printer
2. Miscellneous Machinery
3. Storage tank (for Storing ink, ditution etc.)

FIXED CAPITAL

1. LAND & BUILDING	Rs.	1,51,000.00
2. PLANT & MACHINERY	Rs.	9,75,000.00
3. OTHER FIXED ASSETS	Rs.	65,000.00
TOTAL	Rs.	11,91,000.00

Raw Materials

1. Printing Ink
2. Screen
3. Miscellneous Raw materials

TOTAL WORKING CAPITAL/MONTH

1. RAW MATERIAL	Rs.	60,000.00
2. SALARY & WAGES	Rs.	11,562.50
3. UTILITIES & OVERHEADS	Rs.	36,700.00
TOTAL	Rs.	1,08,262.50

TOTAL CAPITAL INVESTMENT

TOTAL FIXED CAPITAL	Rs.	11,91,000.00
TOTAL WORKING CAPITAL FOR 3 MONTHS	Rs.	3,24,787.50
TOTAL	Rs.	15,15,787.50

TURN OVER/ANNUM

1. Stickers
2. Screen Printing on Plastics
3. Screen Printing on Ceramic Utensils

TOTAL Rs. 24,75,000.00

PROFIT SALES RATIO = PROFIT / SALES X 100 = 23.79 %

RATE OF RETURN = OPERATING PROFIT / T.C.I X 100 = 38.60 %

BREAK EVEN POINT (B.E.P) = 58.16 %

23

Plant Economics of Screen Printing Inks

Rated Plant Capacity = 200 Kgs./Day

LAND & BUILDING (Land Area 750 sq.mtrs.)= Rs. 14,37,500.00

Plant & Machinery

1. Triple roll mill of size - 300mm x 650mm with water cooling - system & 12 HP Motor
2. Planetary Mixer with 5 HP motor, size 200 lit.
3. Varnish Kettle
4. Coal Fired Furnace
5. Material handling equipment. (L.S.)

FIXED CAPITAL

1. LAND & BUILDING	Rs.	14,37,500.00
2. PLANT & MACHINERY	Rs.	3,95,000.00
3. OTHER FIXED ASSETS	Rs.	4,80,000.00
TOTAL	Rs.	23,12,500.00

Raw Materials

1. Pigment (Cadminum Pigment)
2. Tanning Oil
3. Polyamide Resin
4. Wax (Microcrystalline)
5. Packing materials

TOTAL WORKING CAPITAL/MONTH

1. RAW MATERIAL	Rs.	5,09,350.00
2. SALARY & WAGES	Rs.	67,200.00
3. UTILITIES & OVERHEADS	Rs.	49,250.00
TOTAL	Rs.	6,25,800.00

TOTAL CAPITAL INVESTMENT

TOTAL FIXED CAPITAL	Rs.	23,12,500.00
TOTAL WORKING CAPITAL FOR 3 MONTHS	Rs.	18,77,400.00
TOTAL	Rs.	41,89,900.00

TURN OVER/ANNUM

By sale of 60000 kgs of Screen Printing Ink	Rs.1,05,00,000.00

PROFIT SALES RATIO = PROFIT / SALES X 100 = 17.96 %

RATE OF RETURN = OPERATING PROFIT / T.C.I X 100 = 45.01 %

BREAK EVEN POINT (B.E.P) = 46.87 %

24

Plant Economics of Screen Printing on Paper/Cards

Rated Plant Capacity = 10000 Nos/Day

LAND & BUILDING (Land Area 150 Sq.mts) = Rs. 2,10,000.00

Plant & Machinery

1. Complete Desk Top Publishing System (including computer, laser printer, mouse, floppies etc.)
2. Automatic Screen Printing Machine
3. Symphony Air Condition Cooler for Computer.
4. Miscellaneous

FIXED CAPITAL

1. LAND & BUILDING	Rs.	2,10,000.00
2. PLANT & MACHINERY	Rs.	2,82,000.00
3. OTHER FIXED ASSETS	Rs.	1,02,000.00
TOTAL	Rs.	5,94,000.00

Raw Materials

1. Printing Ink
2. Screen
3. Paper For Visiting Cards, Greeting Cards And Other Type.
4. Miscellaneous.

TOTAL WORKING CAPITAL/MONTH

1. RAW MATERIAL	Rs.	1,30,000.00
2. SALARY & WAGES	Rs.	14,125.00
3. UTILITIES & OVERHEADS	Rs.	7,620.00
TOTAL	Rs.	1,51,745.00

TOTAL CAPITAL INVESTMENT

TOTAL FIXED CAPITAL	Rs.	5,94,000.00
TOTAL WORKING CAPITAL FOR 3 MONTHS	Rs.	4,55,235.00
TOTAL	Rs.	10,49,235.00

TURN OVER/ANNUM

1. Paper Cost (Recovery)
2. Visiting Cards,Marriage Cards
   200/100 Greeting Cards, Other

TOTAL	Rs.	28,50,000.00

PROFIT SALES RATIO = PROFIT / SALES X 100 = 25.11 %

RATE OF RETURN = OPERATING PROFIT / T.C.I X 100 = 68.20 %

BREAK EVEN POINT (B.E.P) = 36.87 %

25

Plant Economics of Screen Printing on Cotton Cloth

Rated Plant Capacity = 500 Pcs/Day

LAND & BUILDING (Land Area 500 Sq.mts.) = Rs. 3,65,000.00

Plant & Machinery

1. Printing table
2. Screens
3. Gumming machine
4. Washing Machine
5. Guides, Squeezas, etc.
6. Miscellaneous

FIXED CAPITAL

1. LAND & BUILDING		Rs.	3,65,000.00
2. PLANT & MACHINERY		Rs.	1,97,000.00
3. OTHER FIXED ASSETS		Rs.	1,10,000.00
	TOTAL	Rs.	6,72,000.00

Raw Materials

1. Pieces to be printed
2. Pigment, colour, dyes, etc.
3. Miscellaneous

TOTAL WORKING CAPITAL/MONTH

1. RAW MATERIAL	Rs.	5,20,000.00
2. SALARY & WAGES	Rs.	27,000.00
3. UTILITIES & OVERHEADS	Rs.	39,900.00
TOTAL	Rs.	5,86,900.00

TOTAL CAPITAL INVESTMENT

TOTAL FIXED CAPITAL	Rs.	6,72,000.00
TOTAL WORKING CAPITAL FOR 2 MONTHS	Rs.	11,73,800.00
TOTAL	Rs.	18,45,800.00

TURN OVER/ANNUM

By sale of 1,50,000 pieces	Rs.	93,00,000.00

PROFIT SALES RATIO = PROFIT / SALES X 100 = 20.99 %

RATE OF RETURN = OPERATING PROFIT / T.C.I X 100 = 105.78 %

BREAK EVEN POINT (B.E.P) = 24.27 %

26

Suppliers of Plant & Machinery

Screen Printing
49A, Ramanujam Ngr.
B K Pudur, Coimbatore
Tamil Nadu-641008
Tel : +91 (0) 422822822

Shakti Udyog Ltd.
12, 2nd Cross Rd.
Raja Annamalapuram
Chennai, Tamil Nadu-600028
Tel : +91 (0) 444351554
Fax : +91 (0) 444352148
E-mail :
shaktiudyog@hotmail.com

Grafica Flextronica
Plot No. 92, Survey No. 66
Waliv Fata, Vasai (E)
(Western Rly.), Thane
Maharashtra-401208
Tel : +91 (0) 250455435
Fax : +91 (0) 250455434
E-mail :
grafica@bom3.vsnl.net.in

NSW India Ltd.
Plot No. 43, Sect. 34, EHTP
Gurgaon, Haryana-122001
Tel : +91 (0) 1246371106
Fax : +91 (0) 1246372859
E-mail :
corporate@nswindia.com

Commerce Corporation
A-22, Anurag, Shivram Soc.
Devidayal Rd., Mulund (W)
Mumbai
Maharashtra-400080
Tel : +91 (0) 225676956
Fax : +91 (0) 225676956
E-mail :
kumar812@hotmail.com

Grafica Flextronica
Plot No. 92, Survey No. 66
Waliv Fata, Vasai (E)
(Western Rly.), Thane
Maharashtra-401208
Tel : +91 (0) 250455435
Fax : +91 (0) 250455434
E-mail :
grafica@bom3.vsnl.net.in

ABS Corp.
Nr. Marsden Mills
Rakhial Rd., Ahmedabad
Gujarat-380021
Tel : +91 (0) 792161302
Fax : +91 (0) 792113187

Dipesh Engg. Works
19, Gopal Est., Nr. CTM
Char Rasta, N. H. No. 8
Ahmedabad, Gujarat-380026
Tel : +91 (0) 795855332
E-mail :
deepesh_eng@hotmail.com

Indian Textile Engineers
C-1/B-4, Rd. 'F', Opp. BOB
Phase-I, GIDC, Vatva
Ahmedabad, Gujarat-382445
Tel : +91 (0) 795830192
Fax : +91 (0) 795830579
E-mail : ite@icenet.net

Screenotex Engineers Pvt. Ltd.
Divya Jyoti, Swastik Soc.
Navrangpura, Ahmedabad
Gujarat-380009
Tel : +91 (0) 796565355
Fax : +91 (0) 795712422
E-mail :
screenot@wilnetonline.net

Pratham Technologies Pvt. Ltd.
4/2A, Patil Baug, Daulat Ngr.
Mumbai-Bangalore Highway
Vadgaon (BK), Pune
Maharashtra-411041
Tel : +91 (0) 204355765
Fax : +91 (0) 204352557
E-mail :
varad@pn2.vsnl.net.in

Print Link
325, Mahesh Indl. Est.
Opp. Silver Park, Mira
Bhayander Rd., Mira Rd. (E)
Thane, Maharashtra-401107
Tel : +91 (0) 228118127
Fax : +91 (0) 228110548
E-mail : printink@vsnl.com

Solar Machines Pvt. Ltd.
22-D, Wadia Charities Bldg.
S A Brelvi Rd., Fort, Mumbai
Maharashtra-400001

Tel : +91 (0) 222874642
Fax : +91 (0) 222870470
E-mail :
pulin@bom5.vsnl.net.in

Vaishali Engg. Works
Satam Indl. Est., Ground Flr.
C-Wing, Cardinal Gracious
Rd., Chakala, Andheri (E)
Mumbai, Maharashtra-400099
Tel : +91 (0) 228352105
Fax : +91 (0) 228214276
E-mail :
wvesight@bom3.vsnl.net.in

Winner Screen
R-639, TTC Indl. Area, MIDC
Rabale, Navi Mumbai
Maharashtra-400701
Tel : +91 (0) 227690104
Fax : +91 (0) 227699758
E-mail :
sutsh@bom3.vsnl.net.in

JV Industries
68, Vallalar St., Venketesa Cly.
Pollachi, Tamil Nadu-642001
Tel : +91 (0) 425927457
Fax : +91 (0) 425927520
E-mail :
jvprint@md3.vsnl.net.in

Bonhomie
14/A, Ujagar Indl. Est.
Deonar, Mumbai
Maharashtra-400088
Tel : +91 (0) 225975074
Fax : +91 (0) 225556989
E-mail :
deepak@bonhomie.com

Deluxe Printing Machinery Co.
75/81, Bazargate St. Fort
Mumbai, Maharashtra-400001
Tel : +91 (0) 222618630
Fax : +91 (0) 222618463
E-mail :
deluxe_exp@vsnl.com

Denzil Machine Tools
12, Swamini Indl. Est.
Opp. Bassein Drugs Ltd.
Valiv Taluka, Vasai, Thane
Maharashtra-401202
Tel : +91 (0) 228352105
Fax : +91 (0) 228214276
E-mail :
vewsight@bom3.vsnl.net.in

Enem Electrical & Mechanical Engineers
13, Shirin Chmbrs., 348/50
Samuel St., Mumbai
Maharashtra-400003
Tel : +91 (0) 223426629

Grafica Flextronica
Plot No. 92, Survey No. 66
Waliv Fata, Vasai (E)
(Western Rly.), Thane
Maharashtra-401208
Tel : +91 (0) 250455435
Fax : +91 (0) 250455434
E-mail :
grafica@bom3.vsnl.net.in

Harish Tex-Mach Pvt. ltd.
1/103 Krishna vatika, C.S.C.
Rd. No. 4, B/h Shakti Ngr.
Dahisar (E), Mumbai
Maharashtra-400068
Tel : +91 (0) 228949462
Fax : +91 (0) 228949463
E-mail : harish3@vsnl.com

Kayems Equipment Pvt. Ltd.
205, Dattani Trade Centre
Chandavarkar Lane
Borivali (W), Mumbai
Maharashtra-400092
Tel : +91 (0) 228014376
Fax : +91 (0) 228089609

Kinnari Printing Technologies Pvt. Ltd.
P.O. Box No. 17821, 14, Aroto
House, 3rd Flr., Above Pooja
Blood Bank, P K Rd.
Mulund (W), Mumbai
Maharashtra-400080
Tel : +91 (0) 225907156
Fax : +91 (0) 225681284
E-mail :
kinnari@bom3.vsnl.net.in

Kinnari's Pad Flex
14, Aroto House, 3rd Flr.
Above Pooja Blood bank
P K Rd., Mulund (W), Mumbai
Maharashtra-400080
Tel : +91 (0) 225907156
Fax : +91 (0) 225681284
E-mail :
kinnari@bom3.vsnl.net.in

Mipak Plastics Pvt. Ltd.
16, Khetan Bhavan
198, Jamshedji Tata Rd.
Churchgate, Mumbai
Maharashtra-400020
Tel : +91 (0) 222022942
Fax : +91 (0) 222875994
E-mail :
mppl.mipak@gems.vsnl.net.in

Voltex Electrical Engineers Pvt. Ltd.
B/h Oswal Cancer Hospital
167, Kailash Ngr., Ludhiana
Punjab-141010
Tel : +91 (0) 161670614
Fax : +91 (0) 161673298
E-mail :
info@voltexinternational.com

Lolita Manufacturing Works (Regd.)
9340, Katra Ganga Bishan
Gaushala Marg, Kishan Ganj
NCT of Delhi-110006
Tel : +91 (0) 113621906
Fax : +91 (0) 113621906
E-mail :lolita@lolita
manufacturingworks.com

Metcon Engineers
110, Samrat Bhawan
Ranjit Ngr. Comml. Cmplx.
NCT of Delhi-110008
Tel : +91 (0) 115701038
Fax : +91 (0) 115709527
E-mail :
metcon@del3.vsnl.net.in

Original Sharpline Engineers 2763-64/15, 2nd Flr., Hamilton Rd., Kashmere Gate NCT of Delhi-110006 Tel : +91 (0) 115482366	**Abhishek Print Line** E-26, Nehru Ground, NIT Faridabad, Haryana-121001 Tel : +91 (0) 1295416275 Fax : +91 (0) 1295419983 E-mail : abhishek@nde.vsnl.net.in	**Nutech Graphic Systems** C-269, Sect. 10, Noida Uttar Pradesh-201301 Tel : +91 (0) 1184549608 Fax : +91 (0) 1184549608 E-mail : nutechgraphic@ mantraonline.com
Sharpline Engineers C-71, Laxmi Park, Nangloi NCT of Delhi-110041 Tel : +91 (0) 115945366	**BN Hi Tech Machines Pvt. Ltd.** 363, Indl. Area Phase II Panchkula, Haryana-134113 Tel : +91 (0) 172591884	**Batla Engg. Co.** D-316, Sect. 10, Noida Uttar Pradesh-201301 Tel : +91 (0) 1204547473 Fax : +91 (0) 1204518937 E-mail : batla@vsnl.com

27

Suppliers of Raw Materials

Rita Pad Printing Systems Ltd.
Plot No. 44 & 45, Sect. 18
Gurgaon, Haryana-122015
Tel : +91 (0) 1246343036
Fax : +91 (0) 1246346233
E-mail : info@ritapad.com

Colorinks Pvt. Ltd.
136, Laxmi Bldg.
A M Rd., Kalasipalayam
New Extn., Bangalore
Karnataka-560002
Tel : +91 (0) 802233054
Fax : +91 (0) 802210007
E-mail : sknayak@vsnl.com

Eskay Packagings Pvt. Ltd.
51, Raja Indl. Est.
Mulund (W), Mumbai
Maharashtra-400080
Tel : +91 (0) 225646908
Fax : +91 (0) 225670630
E-mail :
kayess@giasbm01.vsnl.net.in

Inks India
14, Glasswala Bldg., 1st Flr.
Turner Rd., Bandra (W)
Mumbai
Maharashtra-400050
Tel : +91 (0) 226402574
Fax : +91 (0) 226452614

MOK Enterprises
G-30, Kothari Indl. Est.
New Lik Rd., Andheri (W)
Mumbai
Maharashtra-400053
Tel : +91 (0) 226300907
Fax : +91 (0) 226300908

Rainbow Ink & Varnish Manufacturing Company Ltd.
133-C, Vakola
Santacruz (E), Mumbai
Maharashtra-400055
Tel : +91 (0) 226183974
Fax : +91 (0) 226116704
E-mail :
rainboink@bom3.vsnl.net.in

Sericol India Pvt. Ltd.
Gala No.2, Super Processor
Compound, Lal Bag Indl. Est.
Chivda, Galli, Lal Bag
Mumbai
Maharashtra-400025
Tel : +91 (0) 224157025
Fax : +91 (0) 224157026

United Ink & Varnish Company Ltd.
37/40, Subhash Rd.
Vile Parle (E), Mumbai
Maharashtra-400057
Tel : +91 (0) 228366020
Fax : +91 (0) 228381337
E-mail :
uninkvar@gjasbm01.vsnl.net.in

Lavanya Printing Pvt. Ltd.
95, SIDCO Indl. Est.
Thirumazisal, Chennai
Tamil Nadu-602107
Tel : +91 (0) 446290396

Saboo-Berlac Ltd.
Plot No. 81, Phase-II
Indl. Area, Chandigarh
(UT)-160002
Tel : +91 (0) 172652559
Fax : +91 (0) 172652302
E-mail : sbl@glide.net.in

Jaypee Industries Pvt. Ltd.
J-86, Sarita Vihar
NCT of Delhi-110044
Tel : +91 (0) 116972106
Fax : +91 (0) 116972167

Gopani Product Systems
104, Kashiparekh Cmplx.
Swastik Cross Rd.
B/h Bhagwati Chmbr.,C G Rd.
Navrangpura, Ahmedabad
Gujarat-380009
Tel : +91 (0) 796441972
Fax : +91 (0) 796441951
E-mail :
gopani@wilnetonline.net

Fluid Air Filter Systems
G/3, Dev Darshan Cmplx.
Nr. G B Shah College
Vasna, Ahmedabad
Gujarat-380007
Tel : +91 (0) 796633216
Fax : +91 (0) 796633216
E-mail : fafs@sify.com

Multimetal Industries
46, GIDC Est., Makarpura
Vadodara, Gujarat-390010
Tel : +91 (0) 265643587
Fax : +91 (0) 265641060

Essma Felts Pvt. Ltd.
4th Milestone, G T Karnal Rd.
Panipat, Haryana-132103
Tel : +91 (0) 174239327
Fax : +91 (0) 174235456
E-mail : essma@vsnl.com/
essma@palcom.net

Britomatics Engineers Pvt. Ltd.
C-9, Nand Dham Indl. Est.
Marol, Andheri (E), Mumbai
Maharashtra-400059
Tel : +91 (0) 228505834
Fax : +91 (0) 228504999
E-mail :
britomatics@vsnl.com

Haver Standard India Pvt. Ltd.
Standard House, 83
M Karve Marg, P.O. Box No.
20, Mumbai
Maharashtra-400002
Tel : +91 (0) 222060016
Fax : +91 (0) 222086915
E-mail :
hastmesh@bom3.vsnl.net.in

Sharpenn Technologies Pvt. Ltd.
P.O. Box No. 19
Shanmugananda, D-56,
MIDC, B/h London Pilsner
Nerul, Navi Mumbai
Maharashtra-400706
Tel : +91 (0) 227907201
Fax : +91 (0) 227907205
E-mail :
subra@bom3.vsnl.net.in

Dipti Wire Products
24, Sabusiddick Rd.
BMC Bldg. No.4
Nr. Carnac Bridge, Mumbai
Maharashtra-400001
Tel : +91 (0) 222625816
Fax : +91 (0) 222612133
E-mail : diptiwireproducts
@hotmail.com

Dyna Filters Pvt. Ltd.
98/A5, Dyna House
Hadapsar Indl. Est., Pune
Maharashtra-411013
Tel : +91 (0) 20673705
Fax : +91 (0) 20677955
E-mail :
dynafilt@pn2.vsnl.net.in

Georg Fischer Disa Ltd.
40/1A, Basappa Cmplx.
Lavelle Rd., Bangalore
Karnataka-560001
Tel : +91 (0) 802274320
Fax : +91 (0) 802274936
E-mail :
gfdisain@blr.vsnl.net.in

Industrial Enterprises
25, N R Rd., Bangalore
Karnataka-560002
Tel : +91 (0) 802232752

AG Filters
New No. 247, (Old No. 119)
Opp. IGP Ltd., Angappa
Naicken St., Chennai
Tamil Nadu-600001
Tel : +91 (0) 445357423
Fax : +91 (0) 445350960
E-mail : aone@eth.net

Bharat Heavy Electricals Ltd. Boiler Auxiliaries Plant
Indira Gandhi Indl. Cmplx.
Ranipet, Tamil Nadu-632406
Tel : +91 (0) 417241117
Fax : +91 (0) 417241102
E-mail :
csrao@bhelrpt.co.in

C&R Fab Media Pvt. Ltd.
28, 2nd Flr., Palika Bazar
G T Rd., Ghaziabad
Uttar Pradesh-201001
Tel : +91 (0) 1204723715
Fax : +91 (0) 1204719567
E-mail :
crfab@del3.vsnl.net.in

Woollen Textile Industries
G.P.O. Box No. 252
Kolkata, West Bengal-700001
Tel : +91 (0) 332484163
Fax : +91 (0) 332487057
E-mail : wti@cal2.vsnl.net.in

SAF Filter Pvt. Ltd.
34,C R Avenue, Kolkata
West Bengal-700012
Tel : +91 (0) 332376168
Fax : +91 (0) 332373604
E-mail :
safilterpltd@vsnl.com

Varun Wire Products
2-4-495, Door No. 513
Ramgopalpet, Secunderabad
Andhra Pradesh-500003
Tel : +91 (0) 406217322
Fax : +91 (0) 407896218

Gemini Jaliwala
3459-60/10, Gali Bajrang Bali
Chawri Bazar
NCT of Delhi-110006
Tel : +91 (0) 113263660
Fax : +91 (0) 113251676

Vividh Perforators & Agencies
20, Ground Flr.
Nr. Priyadarshini Vihar
P.N. Bank Enclave
NCT of Delhi-110092
Tel : +91 (0) 113233994
Fax : +91 (0) 113233994
E-mail :
vividhp@nda.vsnl.net.in

Jagadamba Enterprises
29, Jay Somnath Soc.
Nr. Aproach Bus Stand
Thakkarnagar Rd.
Bapunagar, Ahmedabad
Gujarat-380024
Tel : +91 (0) 792741288

Shreeji Screen & Filters
8-D-2 Eltee Apts.
Saibaba Ngr., Borivali (W)
Mumbai
Maharashtra-400092
Tel : +91 (0) 228634214
Fax : +91 (0) 228649742
E-mail :
filter@bom5.vsnl.net.in

Atlas Industries
A-8/1, Indl. Est.
Sanathnagar, Hyderabad
Andhra Pradesh-500018
Tel : +91 (0) 403706651
Fax : +91 (0) 407713248

Tirupati Wire Screen & Perforators
5-1-519, 2nd Flr., Hill St.
Secunderabad
Andhra Pradesh-500003
Tel : +91 (0) 407710371
Fax : +91 (0) 407710371

Haver Standard India Pvt. Ltd.
Standard House, 83
M Karve Marg, P.O.
Box No. 20, Mumbai
Maharashtra-400002
Tel : +91 (0) 222060016
Fax : +91 (0) 222086915
E-mail :
hastmesh@bom3.vsnl.net.in

Grafica Flextronica
Plot No. 92, Survey No. 66
Waliv Fata, Vasai (E)
(Western Rly.), Thane
Maharashtra-401208
Tel : +91 (0) 250455435
Fax : +91 (0) 250455434
E-mail :
grafica@bom3.vsnl.net.in

Kishor E Formed Products Pvt. Ltd.
F-93, MIDC, Satpur
Nasik, Maharashtra-422007
Tel : +91 (0) 253350895
Fax : +91 (0) 253351795
E-mail :
contact@kishor-ef.com

Kristeel Shinwa Industries Ltd.
Krislon House, Saki Vihar Rd.
Saki Naka, Mumbai
Maharashtra-400072
Tel : +91 (0) 228575567
Fax : +91 (0) 228574707
E-mail : kristeel@vsnl.com

Nickel Screens & Co.
Jhaveri House, 4th Flr.
348, Abdul Rehman St.
Mumbai Maharashtra-400003
Tel : +91 (0) 223424911
Fax : +91 (0) 223427468
E-mail :
niscreen@vsnl.com

Sans Fibres & Chemicals Pvt. Ltd.
119, Ravikiran Est.
Link Rd., Near Monginis
Factory, Andheri (W), Mumbai
Maharashtra-400595
Tel : +91 (0) 226333420
Fax : +91 (0) 226364369
E-mail :
san@bom3.vsnl.net.in

Prime Steels
Inside P&S Bank Bldg.
3482/5, Chowk Hauz Qazi
NCT of Delhi-110006
Tel : +91 (0) 113266402
Fax : +91 (0) 117459179

DK Enterprise
C/17, Purshottam Est.
Nr. Cozy Hotel, Ranipur Patia
Narol, Ahmedabad
Gujarat-382405
Tel : +91 (0) 795323471
Fax : +91 (0) 795391330

Mihir Industries
C-1-B, 245/3, GIDC Est.
Umbergaon, Gujarat-396171
Tel : +91 (0) 2635463573

Birla 3M Ltd.
6th Flr., Raheja Paramount
138, Residency Rd.
Bangalore
Karnataka-560025
Tel : +91 (0) 802231414
Fax : +91 (0) 802231450

Ruhi Industries
No. 78, Magadi Main Rd.
Bangalore
Karnataka-560079
Tel : +91 (0) 803402103
Fax : +91 (0) 803108221
E-mail : ruhiind@yahoo.com

Chemech Engineers Co-op. Industrial Soc. Ltd.
229-230, DSIDC Sheds
Phase-I Okhla Indl. Area
NCT of Delhi-110020
Tel : +91 (0) 116815044
Fax : +91 (0) 116818317

Chitra Glue
E-131/B, Nr. PNB, Shastri
Ngr., NCT of Delhi-110052
Tel : +91 (0) 113651861

Gems Arcade Inc.
P.O. Box No. 6090
205, Reshabh Shree House
Comml. Cmplx., Ranjit Ngr.
NCT of Delhi-110008
Tel : +91 (0) 115701658
Fax : +91 (0) 115708963

Rajendra Adhesives Industries
160, G T Rd., Shahdara
NCT of Delhi-110032
Tel : +91 (0) 112116163

RR Thanik & Co.
A-796, Shastri Ngr.
NCT of Delhi-110052
Tel : +91 (0) 117773296

Vijay Adhesives Industries
6, Friends Cly. Indl. Area
St. No. 4, G T Rd., Shahdara
NCT of Delhi-110095
Tel : +91 (0) 112281133

National Adhesives
67/11, D-3, MIDC
Chinchwad, Pune
Maharashtra-411019
Tel : +91 (0) 207472694
Fax : +91 (0) 204111434
E-mail : enkays@vsnl.net.in

Sahyadri Products
28, Vaibhav Indl. Est.
Sion-Trombay Rd., Deonar
Mumbai, Maharashtra-400088
Tel : +91 (0) 225513781
Fax : +91 (0) 225564736
E-mail :
anchor@bom4.vsnl.net.in

Darien Electric Pvt. Ltd.
Type-II/35, Dr. VSI Est.
Chennai, Tamil Nadu-600041
Tel : +91 (0) 444925245
Fax : +91 (0) 444481127
E-mail : avara@vsnl.com

Auchtel Products Ltd.
142/C, 2nd Flr., Victor House
N M Joshi Marg, Lower Parel
Mumbai Maharashtra-400013
Tel : +91 (0) 224933975
Fax : +91 (0) 224939755

Indofil Chemicals Co. Industrial Products Divn.
Nirlon House, Dr. Annie
Besant Rd., Worli, Mumbai
Maharashtra-400025
Tel : +91 (0) 224937391
Fax : +91 (0) 224935667
E-mail :
indofil@giasbm01.vsnl.net.in

Lastra Niraj Pvt. Ltd.
118, MIDC, Andheri (E)
Mumbai, Maharashtra-400093
Tel : +91 (0) 228379069
Fax : +91 (0) 228367654
E-mail :
lastra@bom3.vsnl.net.in

Newstech (I) Pvt. Ltd.
261, Udyog Bhavan
Sonawala Rd., Goregaon (E)
Mumbai
Maharashtra-400025
Tel : +91 (0) 228752494
Fax : +91 (0) 224370004
E-mail :
newstech@vsnl.net.in

NS Chemicals & Consultants Pvt. Ltd.
D-224, Ansa Indl. Est.
Sakinaka, Andheri (E)
Mumbai
Maharashtra-400072
Tel : +91 (0) 228523942
Fax : +91 (0) 228523942

Pidilite Industries Ltd. A Parekh Group Company
Ramkrishna Mandir Rd.
Off Marol Vasanji Rd., P.O.
Box 17411, Andheri (E)
Mumbai
Maharashtra-400059
Tel : +91 (0) 228387240
Fax : +91 (0) 228384989

Pilot Industrial Chemicals
19, Kapadia Chmbrs., 51
D Ratanshi Marg, Mumbai
Maharashtra-400009
Tel : +91 (0) 223438581

RSB Chemical Industries
T-136, MIDC, Bhosari
Pune, Maharashtra-411026
Tel : +91 (0) 207120805
Fax : +91 (0) 207122516
E-mail : rsbchem@vsnl.com

Technova Imaging Systems Ltd.
Laxmi Mills Est.
Off Dr. E Moses Rd.
Mahalaxmi, Mumbai
Maharashtra-400011
Tel : +91 (0) 224983390
Fax : +91 (0) 224950322
E-mail :
corp@technovaworld.com

United Ink & Varnish Company Ltd.
37/40, Subhash Rd.
Vile Parle (E), Mumbai
Maharashtra-400057
Tel : +91 (0) 228366020
Fax : +91 (0) 228381337
E-mail : uninkvar@
gjasbm01.vsnl.net.in

Ashok Gum Guar Industries
Plot No. 236, Nr. New Tel.
Exch., GIDC Est., Naroda
Ahmedabad, Gujarat-
382330
Tel : +91 (0) 792812312

ATE Enterprises Ltd.
Mistry Chember, Nr. Cama
Hotel, Khanpur
Ahmedabad
Gujarat-380001
Tel : +91 (0) 795504032
Fax : +91 (0) 795505694
E-mail :
ateahd@ad1.vsnl.net.in

Hindustan Litho Graphics Co.
45, Maheshwari Indl. Est.
Nr. Maheshwari Mills
Shahibaug Rd.
Ahmedabad
Gujarat-380004
Tel : +91 (0) 795623090
Fax : +91 (0) 795623955
E-mail :
hlitho@rediffmail.com

Sharp Tone Graphics Pvt. Ltd.
B/6, Kapidhwaj Avenue,
Nehru Park, Vastrapur
Ahmedabad
Gujarat-380015
Tel : +91 (0) 796750152
Fax : +91 (0) 796760864

Shidimo Interaux Pvt. Ltd.
6th Flr., J K Tower
Nr. Sub-Jail, Ring Rd.
Surat, Gujarat-395002
Tel : +91 (0) 2618311422
Fax : +91 (0) 2618310860
E-mail :
shidimo@icement.net

Aktive Products
125, Amman Koil St.
Chennai, Tamil Nadu-600079
Tel : +91 (0) 44516627

Asian Reprographics Pvt. Ltd.
115 & 116, SIDCO Indl. Est.
Ambattur, Chennai
Tamil Nadu-600098
Tel : +91 (0) 446251619
Fax : +91 (0) 446251544
E-mail :
asianrepro@vsnl.com

Quality Inorganic Chemicals Pvt. Ltd.
35, Thambuswamy Rd.
Kilpauk, Chennai
Tamil Nadu-600010
Tel : +91 (0) 446427943
Fax : +91 (0) 446427943
E-mail : ranne@vsnl.com

King Chemicals
44 C, Indian Mirror St.
Kolkata
West Bengal-700013
Tel : +91 (0) 332455763
Fax : +91 (0) 332446148
E-mail :
kingchem@cal3.vsnl.net.in

Venus Ethoxyethers Pvt. Ltd.
Plot No. 109-111
Bicholim Indl. Est.
Biocholim, Goa-403504
Tel : +91 (0) 832362337
Fax : +91 (0) 832362257
E-mail :
venus.goa@sma.sril.in

Details of Screen Printing Machinery

Fully auto screen printing machine for round bottles max. Dia 100 mm Multi Colour printing max. 3000 P.H

Fully auto screen printing machine for round caps max. Dia 100 mm Single Colour printing max. 3000 P.H

Semi auto screen printing machine for round cont. max. Dia 150 mm Multi Colour printing max. 3000 P.H

Semi auto screen printing machine for round bottles max. Dia 100 mm Single Colour printing max. 1000 P.H

Manual round screen printing machine max print Size upto 50 kg. cont.

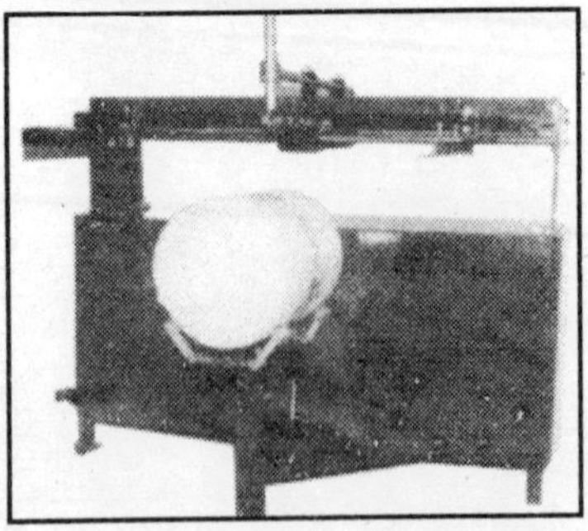

Manual round screen printing machine max print Size upto 2 kg. cont.

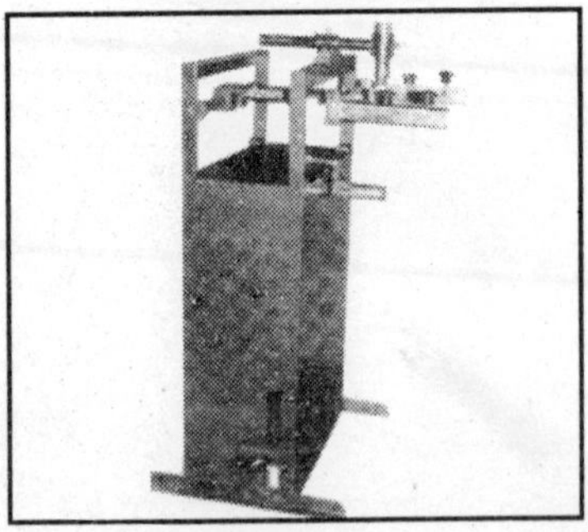

Semi auto printing machine
for round filters in 2 colours

Semi auto pad printing machine
for any type of substrate

Manual pad printing machine
for any shape of objects

C.V. Curing system for flat sheets
maximm speed 6000 P.H.

U.V. Curing system for P.E. tubes or
and round objects

U.V. Curing System for flat sheets
compact size

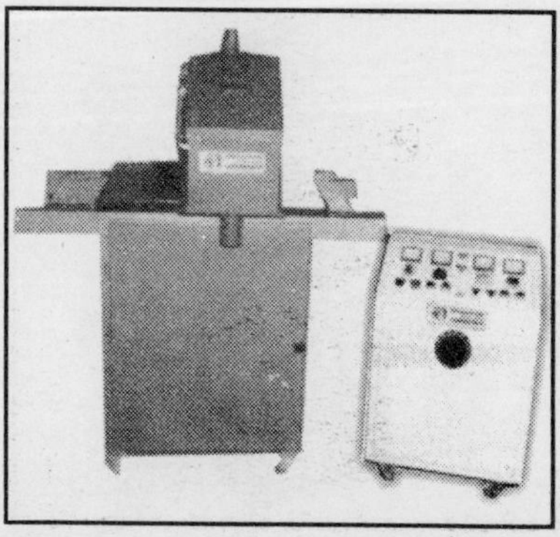

Screen exposing table with U.V. lamp

Control panel for U.V.Lamps

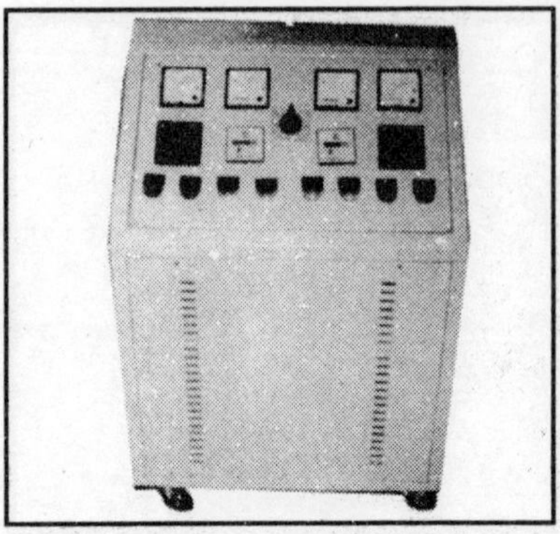

Control gear for U.V. lamps

Manual fabric stretching clamps

Drying racks
suitable for manual screen units

Aluminium Self stretching frames
aluminium tubler frames

Semi auto flat screen printing machine
for flat sheets max. size 16"X22"
Pneumatically operated 600 IM.P.H.

Semi auto flat screen printing machine
with rodeless cylinder max. size 16"X20"
Pneumatically operated 600 IM.P.H.

Semi auto flat screen printing machine
for flat sheets max. size 30"X40"

Manual large format screen printing
machine for flat sheets
max. size 8 feet X 4 feet

Manual vacuum table

T-Shirts printing machine

Courtesy. **Abhishek Print line**

E-26, Nehru Ground, N.I.T., Faridabad - 121001

117. MANUFACTURE OF TIN CONTAINERS
118. MANUFACTURE OF STORAGE TANKS, PRESSURE VESSELS, HEAT EXCHANGERS
119. MARK II HAND PUMPS
120. MARUTI WORKSHOP CUM - SERVICE STATION
121. MECHANICAL JACKS
122. METAL CUTTING DIE DESIGN
123. METAL CUTTING OF AND GRINDING WHEELS (ABBRASIVE CUTTING WHEELS)
124. METAL HOOKS & CLIPS
125. METAL SEPARATION (COPPER, TIN, LEAD) FROM SPENT WASH ACID
126. METALLIC RING JOINTS
127. METALLIC GASKET (SPIRAL WOUND)
128. MICROVEE & ABSOLUTE FILTER
129. MICROWAVE OVEN
130. MILD STEEL INGOTS
131. MINI STEEL PLANT
132. MODERN VEHICLE WORKSHOP
133. MOPED
134. M.S.HINGES
135. M.S.INGOT AND HR. STEEL STRUCTURALS
136. M.S.INGOT BY INDUCTION FURNACES
137. M.S.PIPES
138. M.S. WELDING ELECTRODE
139. MUFFLERS & SILENCERS FOR THREE WHEELERS
140. NAIL CUTTER WITH FILER & MANICURE
141. NICHROME WIRE
142. NICKEL LINED SCREENS
143. NON-FERROUS ALLOY ROLLING
144. NON-FERROUS FORGING
145. NON-FERROUS FOUNDRY
146. NON PRESSURE
147. INCANDESCENT LAMP
148. NUMBER COMBINATION LOCKS FOR LUGGAGES
149. NUTS & BOLTS
150. PAPER COATED ALUMINIUM AND COPPER WIRE
151. PETROMAX CONTAINER
152. PHOTO ETCHING OF STAINLESS STEEL PLATES
153. PIPE GALVANIZING PLANT
154. PISTON RING-AUTOMOBILE
155. PLANT PROTECTION EQUIPMENTS
156. PLATINUM LABORATORY APPARATUS
157. PRESSURE COOKER & ALUMINIUM UTENSILS
158. PRESSURE COOKER (ALUMINIUM)
159. PRESSURE DIE CASTING
160. PRINTED ALUMINIUM COLLAPSIBLE TUBES
161. PRINTED TIN CONTAINERS
162. PRINTING PRESS (CYLINDER MACHINE)
163. PUMPS FOR CHEMICAL INDUSTRY (SPECIAL)
164. RAILWAY SLEEPERS (M.S.)
165. RAZOR TWIN BLADE
166. R.C.C SPUN PIPES
167. RECONDITIONING OF M.S. DRUMS/BARRELS
168. RE-ROLLING COPPER AND BRASS SHEET AND RODS
169. RE-ROLLING MILLS
170. RESIN COATED SAND
171. RESIN CORED SOFT SOLDER WIRES
172. ROLLING MILL (BY INDUCTION FURNACE) & MANUFACTURE OF BARS, ANGLES, SQUARES, TUBES AND OTHERS
173. ROLLER BEARING & FORGING
174. ROLLING OF STAINLESS STEEL PATTA
175. RUBBER INSULATED PLIERS (HAND TOOLS)
176. RUBBING COMPOUND FOR AUTOMOBILES
177. SCIENTIFIC LABORATORY EQUIPMENTS
178. SCOOTER ASSEMBLING
179. SECONDARY LEAD EXTRAC -TION BY SCRAP BATTERY PLATES,PIPES & SHEET
180. SEAMLESS M.S. TUBES & PIPES
181. SELF TAPPING STEEL SCREW
182. SEWING NEEDLES
183. S.G. IRON & ALLOY STEEL
184. SHEET METAL PRODUCTS, (FERROUS/NON-FERROUS)
185. SHIP/MARINE CONTAINER
186. SHOCK ABSORBERS
187. SHOE EYELETS
188. SHOT AND GRITS BY AUTOMIZATION PROCESS
189. SHOVELS
190. SILICO MANGANESE ALLOYS
191. SILENCERS (MUFFLERS) EXHAUST & TAIL PIPE FOR ALL TYPES OF VEHICLES
192. SINTERED BEARING
193. SINTERED BUSHES
194. SINTERED METAL PRODUCTS
195. SOFT AND HARD FERRITES
196. SPANNERS
197. SPARK PLUGS
198. STEEL PLANT (ELECTRIC ARC FURNACE BASED- EAF)
199. SPHERIODAL GRAPHITE CAST IRON
200. SPRAY DRYER
201. STAINLESS STEEL HINGES
202. STAINLESS STEEL SHEET ROLLING TO PRODUCE STAINLESS STEEL UTENSILS
203. STAINLESS STEEL UTENSILS
204. STAPLE PINS,PAPER PIN, GEM CLIPS ETC.
205. STEEL CASTINGS
206. STEEL CHAIN
207. STEEL FOUNDRY
208. STEEL FURNITURES AND ELECTRICAL APPLIANCES
209. STEEL PLANT (MINI)
210. STEEL RODS AND COILS FROM SCRAPS
211. STEEL ROLLING MILL
212. STEEL STRIPS (COLD ROLLED) SILICON WITH GRAIN RIENTED FOR ELECTRIC USE
213. STEEL TRANSMISSION LINE TOWERS & ROLLING MILL TO PRODUCE STEEL SECTION
214. STEEL FURNITURES AND ELECTRICAL APPLIANCES
215. STEEL WIRE DRAWING AND GALVANIZING
216. STEEL WOOL
217. SUBMERGED ARC WELDED PIPES
218. SUBMERSIBLE PUMP MANUFACTURING
219. SUPER ENAMELLED COPPER WIRE
220. THREE WHEELERS
221. TIE-ROD ENDS
222. TIN CONTAINERS
223. TOOLROOM AND SHEET METAL PRODUCTS
224. TRACTOR TRAILERS
225. TRANSMISSION POWER FITTING
226. TUBULAR POLES
227. SUPER ENAMELLED COPPER WIRES
228. TUBULAR POLES FOR ELECTRICAL TRANSMISSION (BY FABRICATION PROCESS)
229. TUBULAR POLES OF M.S. & HIGH TENSILE STEEL
230. VACUUM CLEANERS
231. VACUUM FLASK (STAINLESS STEEL)
232. VALVES FOR REFRIGERA TION AND AIR-CONDITION
233. VEHICLE WELDING & PAINTING
234. VENETION BLIND
235. WASHING MACHINES (AUTOMATIC & COMPUTERISED)
236. WATER CONTROLLER (AUTOMATIC)
237. WATCH STRAPS/CHAINS/ BRACELETS/BELT BRASS & STAINLESS STEEL
238. WATER COOLERS
239. WELDED WIRE MESH
240. WELDING ELECTRODES
241. WICK STOVES
242. WIND MILL WINDOW FRAME (FERROUS & NON-FERROUS)
243. WRIST WATCH

359. DI ETHYL OXALATE
360. DI METHYL ORTHOPHTHALATE
361. DI-METHYL PHTHALATE
362. DICLOFENAC GEL
363. DIOCTYL PHTHALATE (DOP)
364. DI PHENYL GLYCERINE
365. DI PHENYL OXIDE
366. DINITRO-CHLORO BENZENE
367. DISTILLED WATER
368. DODECYL BENZENE SULPHONATE
369. DUSTLESS CHALK
370. EDTA & ITS SALTS
371. ELECTROLESS NICKEL PLATING ON PLASTICS
372. ENDOSULFAN
373. EPOXY RESIN BASED COMPOUND
374. ETHYL ACETATE
375. EHTYL ETHER
376. ETHYL ALCOHOL (POTABLE LIQUOR)
377. ETHYL HEXANOL
378. EXTRACTION OF ESSENTIAL OILS BY SUGAR CRITICAL FLUID (CARBON DIOXIDE) METHOD FROM FLOWERS, HERBAL & SPICES
379. FERRIC ALUM
380. FERRO CHROME LIGNO SULPHONATE
381. FERRO MANGANESE
382. FERRO SILICONE
383. FERRO VANADIUM FROM VANADIUM SLUDGE
384. FERROUS SILICATE
385. FERROUS SULPHATE
386. FERTILIZER FROM ANIMAL BLOOD & LEATHER WASTE
387. FLUORESCENT TUBE LIGHT POWDER
388. FOAMED PVC COMPOUNDING & ITS PRODUCTS
389. FORMALDEHYDE
390. FRACTIONAL DISTILLATION OF D.M.O (DEMENTHOLIZED OIL)
391. FRACTIONAL DISTILLATION OF ESSENTIAL OIL & MEDICINAL PLANT EXTRACT
392. FRICTION DUST (LIQUID & POWDER) FROM CNSL
393. FRUIT FLAVOURS
394. FURFURAL FROM RICE HUSK
395. GARLIC ACID
396. GASKET SHELLAC COMPOUND
397. GEAR OIL
398. GIBBERELLIC ACID
399. GLASS PUTTY
400. GLYCERINE
401. GOSSYPOL (POLY PHENOL) FROM COTTON SEED OIL
402. GUAR GUM POWDER
403. HAIR FIXER (HAIR GEL TYPE)
404. H - ACID
405. HENNA PASTE MAKING
406. HEPTAL DEHYDE
407. HIGH CARBON FERRO CHROME
408. HYDRATED CALCIUM SILICATE BRICK
409. HYDRATED LIME FROM SEA SHELL
410. HYDROCHLORIC ACID
411. HYDRO FLUORIC ACID
412. HYDROGEN PEROXIDE (BY AUTO-OXIDATION PROCESS)
413. ICE PACKS (SOLUTIONS TYPE, WHITE GEL TYPE, VIOLET SEMI SOLID POLYMER TYPE)
414. IMPROVING DROP POINT PARAFFIN WAX FROM 45-50°C TO 75-80°C
415. INDUSTRIAL ALCOHOL
416. INTEGERATED COMPLEX OF EASTER & ALLIED PRODUCTS (D.O.P, D.B.P, ETHYL ACETATE WIRE ENAMEL & CABLE JELLY)
417. IMFL (WHISKY) & COUNTRY LIQUOR
418. IRON OXIDE FOR MAKING FERITTE
419. IRON SULPHIDE
420. JUTE BATCHING OIL
421. KESH KALA TEL (HAIR DYE LOTION) (VASMOL 33, BLACK NITE TYPE)
422. L-LYSINE MONOHYDROCHLORIDE
423. LACTIC ACID FROM WHITE SUGAR BY FERMENTATION PROCESS
424. LDPE GRANULES FROM VIRGIN (LDPE RESIN)
425. LEAD EXTRACTION FROM BATTERY SCRAP
426. LEAD OXIDE (A) LEAD MONOXIDE (B) LEAD TETRA OXIDE (C) GREYLEAD OXIDE
427. LIQUID GLUCOSE & ITS BY PRODUCTS
428. LIQUID OXYGEN BOTTLING PLANT
429. LIQUID SHOE POLISH
430. LIQUID FLOOR POLISH
431. LUBE OIL VISCOSITY IMPROVED FOR P.P.G/P.E.G.
432. LUBRICANTS ASHLESS 100% COMBUSTION
433. MAGNESIUM CARBONATE AND MAGNESIUM BICARMONATE
434. MAGNESIUM HYDROXIDE POWDER
435. MAGNESIUM SILICATE
436. MAGNESIUM SULPHATE
437. MALACHITE GREEN
438. MALEIC ANHYDRIDE
439. MANGANESE SULPHATE
440. MANUFACTURING OF CARBON MONO-OXIDE WATER GAS
441. MENTHOL BOLD CRYSTALS FROM FLAKES
442. MENTHOL CRYSTAL & MENTHA OIL
443. MERCURIC OXIDE
444. METAL PRE-TREATMENT CHEMICALS
445. METHANE GAS BY SODIUM ACETATE & SODA LIME
446. METHYL ACETYL RICINOLATE
447. METOL
448. METOL FROM HYDROQUI-NONE & METHYLAMINE
449. MICANITE
450. MICRO NUTRIENT MIXTURE
451. MINERAL WATER
452. MINERAL WATER AND PET BOTTILNG PLANT
453. MINERAL WATER IN BOTTLES, GLASS AND POUCHES
454. MINI CEMENT PLANT (BY ROTARY KILN PROCESS)
455. MIXED FERTILIZER
456. MOSQUITO & FLIES REPELLENT AGARBATTI (INCENSE STICKS)
457. MONO CHLORO ACETIC ACID
458. MONOCROTOPHOS (TECHNICAL)
459. MOSQUITO COIL
460. MOSQUITO COIL & MAT
461. MOSQUITO MAT
462. MOTHER TINCTURE & BIO CHEMIC MEDICINES
463. NAPHTHALENE & PHENYL (INTEGRATED UNIT)
464. NATURAL MINERAL WATER BY REVERSE OSMOSIS PROCESS
465. NICKEL PLATING BRIGHTNER (PRIMARY OR CARRIER BRIGHTNER & SECONDARY BRIGHTNER)
466. NICKEL SULPHATE
467. NICOTINE FROM TOBACCO WASTE
468. NICOTINE SULPHATE FROM TOBACCO WASTE
469. NITRO BENZENE
470. NITRO CELLULOSE SANDING SEALER/LACQUER
471. NITRO MUSK
472. NITROGEN & OXYGEN GAS PLANT
473. NON-IONIC SURFACTANT (WETTING AGENT)
474. NO-CARB PASTE
475. OCTANOL
476. ORTHO NITRO PHENOL
477. OXALIC ACID FROM MOLASSES
478. OXALIC ACID FROMRICE HUSK
479. OXALIC ACID FROM TREE BARK
470. OXALIC ACID FROM WASTE VEGETABLES
471. OXYGEN GAS PLANT
472. OXYGEN GAS PLANT (AIR SEPERATION METHOD)
473. PARA-AMINO BENZOIC ACID
474. PARA-AMINO PHENOL
475. PARA TOLUENE SULPHONIC ACID
476. PECTIN FROM RAW PAPAYA
477. PERFUME (LEMON & OTHERS)

CRUDE NAPHTHA
570. TRIMETHYL AMMONIUM CHLORIDE
571. TRIPHENYL PHOSPHITE (T.P.P)
572. ULTRAMARINE BLUE (LIQUID)
573. UREA FORMALDEHYDE & MELAMINE FORMALDEHYDE POWDER
574. UNDECYLINIC ACID
575. VINYL ACETATE MONOMER
576. VITAMIN C
577. VITAMIN E
578. WASTE WATER TREATMENT PLANT FOR INDUSTRIAL SECTOR IN INDIA (ONLY MARKER SURVEY)
579. WIRE DRAWING LUBRICANT
580. WIRE ENAMEL
581. XANTHATES
582. YELLOW DEXTRIN
583. ZINC CHLORIDE
584. ZINC OXIDE
585. ZINC PHOSPHATING BY COLD PROCESS
586. ZINC SILICATE
587. ZINC STEARATE
588. ZINC SULPHATE
589. ZINC SULPHATE MONOHYDRATE
590. ACID BLACK
591. AURAMINE'O'
592. AZO DYES STUFF
593. DYE & DYE INTERMEDIATE
594. DYE INTERMEDIATES
595. MALACHITE GREEN
596. METHYLENE BLUE
597. PHTHALOCYANINE BLUE
598. PHTHALOCYANINE BLUE & GREEN
599. REACTIVE DYES
600. SULPHUR BLACK DYE
601. VAT DYES
602. WATER CHILLING PLANT
603. WADDING OIL (100%) FOR WADDING OF COTTON HOSIERY CLOTH IN THE DYEING PROCESS
604. WHITE OIL
605. WAX FLOOR POLISH

ELECTRICAL, ELECTONICS, COMPUTERS AND INFOTECH/IT PROJECTS

606. AIR CONDITIONING
607. ALUMINIUM ALLOY CONDUCTOR
608. ALUMINIUM CABLE
609. ALUMINIUM ELECTROYTIC CAPACITORS
610. AUDIO CASSETTE ASSEMBLING & RECORDING
611. AUDIO CASSETTES DUPLICATING RECORDING
612. AUDIO CASSETTES & AUDIO STUDIO
613. AUDIO CASSETTES PLANE & RECORDED
614. AUDIO MAGNETIC HEADS
615. AUDIO MAGNETIC TAPE
616. AUDIO/VIDEO CASSETTES
617. AUTO BULB/LAMPS
618. AUTOMATIC VOLTAGE STABILIZER
619. BATTERY PLATES
620. BACK OFFICE (Rs. 5000/-)
621. B/W TV & COMPUTER MONITOR PICTURE TUBE
622. BREAD BOARDS
623. CALL CENTRE
624. CAMERA (35 MM)
625. CAPACITORS
626. CARBON ELECTRODE USED FOR BATTERY CELL
627. CARBON POTETIOMETERS
628. CEILING FAN
629. CERAMIC INSULATOR
630. CHILDREN INFOTECH TRAINING INSTITUTE (Rs. 5000/-)
631. CHOKE AND PATTI
632. CHOKE AND STARTER
633. CHOKE USED FOR FLUORESCENT LAMPS
634. COLOUR TELEVISION
635. COLOUR AND BLACK & WHITE TELEVISION
636. COMPACT DISC
637. COMPACT DISC PLAYER (AUDIO/VIDEO)
638. COMPUTER EDUCATION INSTITUTE
639. COMPUTER ASSEMBLY
640. COMPUTER HARDWARE
641. COMPUTER KEYBOARD
642. COMPUTER PERIPHERALS
643. COMPUTER PRINTERS
644. COMPUTER RIBBON
645. COMPUTER RIBBON REINKING OR REFILLING
646. COMPUTER STATIONERY
647. COMPUTER STATIONERY &

IMPORTED HARDWARE PARTS
648. COMPUTER TERMINALS
649. COMPUTERISED WASHING MACHINE (AUTOMATIC)
650. COMPUTER SOFTWARE
651. CONDENSER FOR MOTOR USING MPP FILM
652. CONTENT DEVELOPMENT CENTRE (EOU) (Rs. 5000/-)
653. CONTROL PANEL BOARD
654. COOLING COIL FOR AIR CONDITIONERS
655. COPFER STRIP COIL FROM SCRAP
656. CORDLESS TELEPHONES
657. CYBER CAFE
658. CYBERKIOSK (Rs. 5000/-)
659. DATA PROCESSING CENTRE (Rs. 5000/-)
660. D.C. MICRO MOTORS
661. D.G.SETS
662. DISH ANTENNA AND CABLE T.V. NETWORK EQUIPMENT
663. DISTRIBUTION TRANSFORMERS & REPAIRS
664. DOMESTIC ELECTRICAL APPLIANCES- ROOM COOLER, WASHING MACHINE, WATER HEATER, ELECTRIC ROOM HEATER
665. E-SCHOOL
666. E-COMMERCE/BUSINESS
667. ELECTRIC ENERGY METER
668. ELECTRIC FANS
669. ELECTRIC HORN FOR AUTOMOBILE
670. ELECTRIC LAMP/GLS (INCANDESCENT LAMP)
671. ELECTRIC MIXER
672. ELECTRIC MOTORS UP TO 10 HP. REWINDING OF ALL TYPES OF MOTORS WATER PUMPS
673. ELECTRIC MOTOR WINDING (FOR FAN, MIXIES, ETC.)
674. ELECTRIC STEAM IRON
675. ELECTRICAL APPLIANCES
676. ELECTRICAL FIXTURES
677. ELECTRICAL STAMPING
678. ELECTROLYTIC CAPACITORS
679. ELECTROMAGNETIC RELAY
680. ELECTRONIC BALAST/CHOK
681. ELECTRICAL CHOKE
682. ELECTRONIC DIGITAL WATCHES
683. ELECTRONIC DIGITAL WEIGHING MACHINE
684. ELECTRONIC FIRE ALARM
685. ELECTRONIC GAS STOVE LIGHTERS
686. ELECTRONIC PRESSURE INDICATORS, ELECTRICALS, ELECTRONIC LIQUID LEVEL INDICATORS, ELECTRONIC TEMPERATURE INDICATOR, DIGITAL TACHOMETER
687. ELECTRONIC TELEPHONE INSTRUMENTS
688. ELECTRONIC TOYS
689. ELECTRONIC WATCHES & CLOCKS
690. FAX MACHINES
691. F.H.P MOTORS
692. FLOPPY DISKETTES
693. FLUORESCENT LAMP STARTER
694. FLUORESCENT TUBULAR

Above all the Detailed Project Reports are available at *"ENGINEERS INDIA RESEARCH INSTITUTE"*. 4449, Nai Sarak (D), Main Road Delhi - 110 006
● Ph : 91-11-23918117, 2391 6431, 23840361, 31082370 ●Fax : 91-11-2391 6431
●E-Mail : eirisidi@bol.net.in

LAMPS WITH INTRODUCTION TO MERCURY VAPOUR LAMP
695. FRANCHISEE COMPUTER EDUCATION CENTRE (Rs. 5000)
696. GAS DETECTOR (L.P.G)
697. GENERATOR SET & PUMP SETS
698. GENERATOR (BATTERY OPERATED)
699. GIS SERVICE CENTRE (GEOGRAPHICAL INFORMATION SYSTEMS)
700. HARDWARE FITTING FOR TRANSMISSION LINE OVERHEAD LINE MATERIAL
701. HEADERS FOR TRANSISTOR ICS SEMI CONDUCTOR
702. H.T & L.T INSULATORS
703. H.T & M.V INDUSTRIAL CUBICAL SWITCH BOARD
704. INFORMATION MOVING DISPLAY (L.E.D TYPE)
705. INSURANCE CLAIM PROCESSING CENTRE (EOU) (Rs. 5000/-)
706. INTEGRATED CIRCUITS
707. INTERNET BASED STOCK TRADING (Rs. 5000/-)
708. INTERNET SERVICE PROVIDER (I.S.P.)
709. JELLY FILLED TELEPHONE CABLES
710. LAP TOP COMPUTERS
711. LEAD ACID BATTERIES
712. LEAD ACID BATTERY PLATES AND ASSEMBLING OF BATTERY
713. LEGAL TRANSCRIPTION & SECRETARIAL SERVICES CENTER (EOU)(Rs. 5000/-)
714. LIGHT EMITTING DIODES (L.E.D)
715. LINEAR ICS TRAINER KIT
716. LOUD SPEAKER
717. L.T TRANSFORMER REPAIRING
718. MEDICAL TRANSCRIPTION CENTRE
719. METAL FILM RESISTORS
720. METALLISED POLYPROPYLENE, POLYESTER FILM CAPACITOR
721. MICA BASE ELECTRONIC COMPONENTS
722. MICA PAPER WASTE PAPER FROM MICA WASTE
723. MICRO PROCESSORS TRAINER KITS BASED ON MICRO PROCESSORS
724. MINI COMPUTER (PERSONAL COMPUTER)
725. MINIATURE CIRCUIT BREAKER (M.C.B)
726. MINIATURE WATCH BATTERIES (BUTTON CELL)
727. MIXER/GRINDER (MIXI)
728. MONO CHROME COMPUTER MONITOR
729. MOTOR START ELECTROLYTIC CAPACITOR
730. MULTI LAYER P.C.B
731. MULTIPLE RELAY FOR LOW VOLTAGE
732. NEON INDICATOR
733. NEON SIGN MANUFACTURE
734. OPTICAL FIBRE CABLES
735. ON LINE SHOPPING MALL (Rs. 5000/-)
736. OPTO MECHANICAL & ELECTRICAL EQUIPMENTS
737. PHOTO COLOUR LAB
738. PICTURE TUBE (B/W)
739. PLAIN PAPER COPIER
740. PLASTIC FILM CAPACITORS
741. POLYESTER CAPACITORS
742. PORTABLE GENERATOR SET
743. PORTAL
744. PORTABLE TELEVISION(TV)
745. POWER CAPACITORS
746. POWER INVERTERS
747. POWER PLANT
748. POWER TRANSFORMERS UP TO 600 KVA
749. PRINTED CIRCUIT BOARD
750. PVC WIRES & CABLES
751. RE-CONDITIONING OF PICTURE TUBE
752. RESIN CAST CT & PT (1 KV)
753. SEMI CONDUCTOR DEVICE
754. SEMI CONDUCTORS FOR TRANSISTORS & DIODES
755. SETTING UP OF A VIDEO STUDIO
756. SMOKE DETECTORS
757. SOLAR CELLS
758. SOLAR MODULES
759. SOLAR PHOTO VOLTAIC SYSTEM
760. SOLDER FLUXES
761. SOLAR WATER HEATING PANELS
762. STEEL FURNITURE & ELECTRICAL APPLIANCES
763. STEREO AMPLIFIERS
764. STEREO CASSETTE RECORDERS/PLAYERS
765. STREET LIGHT FITTINGS SURGE SUPPRESSOR
766. TANTALUM CAPACITORS
767. TEFLON COATED ELECTRIC CABLE
768. TELEMEDICINE (DISTANCE HEALTH CARE) (Rs. 5000/-)
769. TELEPHONE CORD/CABLE
770. TELEPHONE (PUSH BUTTON TYPE)
771. TELEPHONE (PUSH BUTTON & CORDLESS)
772. TELEVISION (CTV & B/W)
773. TELEVISION (3-D)
774. TELEVISION DEFLECTION COMPONENTS
775. TELEVISION SIGNAL BOOSTERS
776. TELEVISION TUNERS
777. TRACTION BATTERIES
778. TRAINING INSTITUTE OF MEDICAL TRANSCRIPTION
779. TRANSFORMER FOR B/W TV
780. TRANSFORMER FOR VOLTAGE STABILIZER & E.H.T
781. TRANSMISSION POWER LINE FITTING
782. TRANSMISSION TOWER FITTING
783. TV AUDIO EQUIPMENT CABINETS & THEIR ASSEMBLING UNIT
784. UN-INTERRUPTED POWER SUPPLY (U.P.S)
785. VARIABLE FREQUENCY
786. VARIABLE VOLTAGE A.C. DRIVE
787. VIDEO CASSETTES (COMPLETE MANUFACTURING & ASSEMBLING)
788. VIDEO CASSETTES RECORDER (V.C.R)
789. VIDEO FILM STUDIO
790. VOLTAGE REGULATOR FOR AUTOMOBILES
791. VOLTAGE STABILIZERS
792. VOLTAGE STABLIZER & T.V. GAIN BOOSTER
793. WAX AND CHEMICAL COATED, BRAIDED TINSEL WIRE
794. WEBSITE DESIGN & E-MAIL REGISTERING
795. WELDING ELECTRODES
796. WIND ENERGY POWER PROJECT (10 MW)
796A WIRES (METAL)

FOOD, AGRO FOOD, PROCESSED FOOD, AGRO PLANTATION, CULTIVATION, FARMING, DAIRY/MILK, TOBACCO/PAN MASALA, BREWERY & DISTILLERY, EDIBLE OILS, EOU FOOD PRODUCTS AND ALLIED PRODUCTS

797. ALCOHOLIC BEVERAGES & VENEGAR FROM COCONUT WATER
798. ALCOHOL DRINKS FROM ETHYL ALCOHOL BY MIXING OF VARIOUS FLAVOURS
799. ANTI SCALE COMPOUND FOR ADDING INTO SUGAR JUICE BOILING
800. APPLE JUICE CONCENTRATED & DEHYDRATED FRUIT & VEGETABLES
801. ARTIFICIAL FISH MEAL FOR POULTRY FEED
802. AUTOMATIC BISCUIT PLANT
803. BABY CEREAL FOOD AND MILK POWDER
804. BACTERIA FOR CANE JUICE
805. BAKER'S YEAST
806. BAKERY INDUSTRY
807. BANANA PUREE
808. BEER & WINE
809. BEER PLANT (BREWERY)
810. BIDI
811. BIDI & CIGARETTE
812. BISCUIT PLANT

813. BREAD (AUTOMATIC PLANT)
814. BLACK PEPPER (SPICES)
815. BREAD AND BISCUITS
816. BREEDING FARM
817. BROILER CHICKEN
819. BUTTON MUSHROOM CULTIVATION & PROCESSING
820. CANNING OF RASAGULLAS IN METAL CANS
821. CAFFEIN FROM TEA WASTE
822. CANNING OF FRUITS & VEGETABLES
823. CASEIN AND BY-PRODUCTS
824. CASHEW FRUIT JUICE FROM CASHEW FRUIT APPLE
825. CASHEWNUT KERNEL EXTRACTION FROM CASHEWNUT FRUIT
826. CASHEWNUT SHELL LIQUID & KERNEL PROCESSING
827. CASHEW FENI
828. CATECHEU (BY CHEMICAL PROCESS)
829. CATTLE FEED FROM TAPIOCA
830. CHEWING & BUBBLE GUM
831. CHICKEN/SHEEP MEAT PROCESSING
832. CHOCOLATE (MILK)
833. CIGARETTE AND BEEDIES
834. COCOA BUTTER FROM COCOA MASS
835. COCONUT PRODUCTS & BY PRODUCTS PROCESS COMPLEX
836. COLD/SOFT DRINKS
837. COLLECTION OF MILK AND MILK MAKING POWDER
838. COLLECTION OF MILK AND PACKING IN POLYTHENE POUCH (1/2 KG.1 KG. & 2 KG.)
839. CONDENSED MILK (SWEETNED)
840. CONFECTIONERY INDUSTRY (TOFFEE & CANDY, SEMI-AUTOMATIC PLANT)
841. COUNTRY LIQUOR FROM MOLASSES
842. CIGARETTE
843. DAIRY FARM AND DAIRY (MILK) PRODUCTS (PASTEURISED MILK, BUTTER, GHEE, PANEER)
844. DAIRY FARM TO PRODUCE MILK & PACKING IN POUCHES (50%) & CAN(50%)
845. DAIRY FOR MILK PROCESSING
846. DAIRY FARM (BUFALO)
847. DAL (PULSE) MILL UNIT
848. DEHYDRATION OF CARROT & GARLIC
849. DEHYDRATION & CANNING OF FRUITS & VEGETABLES
850. DEHYDRATION OF FIGS
851. DEHYDRATION OF FRUITS AND VEGETABLES
852. DEHYDRATED ONIONS AND ONION POWDER
853. DRY ICE BY BREAKING OF AIR
854. DRYING OF RED CHILLIES, HALDI, DHANIA, AND GREEN PEAS
855. EGG POWDER (40,000 EGGS PROCESSING PER DAY)
856. EXPORT OF PROCESSED FOODS AND MARINE PRODUCTS
857. FISH CANNING & POUCHING
859. FISH FARMING (PRAWN & OTHER MARINE PRODUCTS)
860. FISH MEAL
861. FLOUR MILL AND MUSTARD OIL
862. FOOD COLOUR & ORASTED GROUNDNUT GRAM PEAS, ETC IN POUCHES
863. FROG LEGS PROCESSING
864. FROZEN MEATS PROCESSING
865. FOOD FLAVOURS (WHISKY) VODKA, GRAPE, BUTTER SCOTCH)
866. FOOD PRODUCTS COMPLEX (DEHYDRATED ONIONS, GARLIC POWDER & FLAKES, CATTLE FEED, TOMATO POWDER, TOMATO PRODUCTS, CANNED FRUITS & VEGETABLES, TOMATO PURE, GROUN NUT OIL, REFIND OIL, DEHYDRATED GRAPES, BANANA POWDER & WAFFERS)
867. FRUIT JUICE, JAM, JELLIES & ALLIED PRODUCTS
868. FRUIT JUICE, PICKLES PROCESSING AND CANNING
869. FRUIT JUICE MAKING & PACKING IN PLASTIC CONTAINER/POUCHES
870. FRUIT PROCESSING (JAM & JELLIES)
871. FRUIT PULP & JUICE CONCENTRATES
872. FRUIT & VEGETABLE DRYING (FREEZE DRYING METHOD)
873. GOAT & SHEEP FARMING
874. GRAM DALL/PULSE MILL
875. GRAPE DEHYDRATION
876. HARD BOILED CANDY (TOFFEE & CANDY)
877. HERBAL CIGARETTES
878. HONEY PROCESSING & PACKAGING
879. ICE CREAM OF DIFFERENT FLAVOURS
880. ICE CREAM STABILIZER
881. ICE MAKING PLANT
882. INDIAN MADE FOREIGN LIQUOR (I.M.F.L)
883. INSTANT FOOD (IDLI MIX, DOSA MIX, GULAB JAMUN MIX)
884. INSTANT FOOD (INSTANT FOOD & FAST FOOD PARLOUR)
885. INSTANT NOODLES
886. INSTANT TEA
887. INSTANT TEA FROM BLACK TEA
888. INTEGERATED STARCH BAKING POWDER/YEAST INDUSTRY
889. IODIZED SALT
890. IODIZED SALT (ORDINARY MOISTURE-LESS/FREE FLOWING IN PLASTIC BAGS AND CONTAINERS)
891. JAM, JELLIES, FRUIT JUICE & ALLIED PRODUCTS
892. KATHA AND CUTCH
893. KHANDSARI SUGAR
894. KHANDSARI SUGAR & IMFL
895. LACTIC ACID FROM WHITE SUGAR BY FERMENTATION PROCESS
896. LACTOSE & BY PRODUCTS PROCESSING FROM MILK
897. LIQUID GLUCOSE AND ITS BYE PRODUCTS
898. MACRONI AND VERMICILLI
899. MALT EXTRACTION FROM BARLEY
900. MANGO PROCESSING (MANGO PULP, JUICE & SLICES)
901. MAYUR BRAND TYPE CHEWING TOBACCO
902. MINERAL WATER
903. MILK PRESERVATION & MARKETING TO WHOLE SELLERS (INPOUCH PACKING BY UHT TECHNOLOGY)
904. MILK PROCESSING AND PACKAGING OF MILK PRODUCTS
905. MILK PRODUCTS (CASEIN, LACTOSE, GHEE & WHEY POWDER)
906. MILK TOFFEE
907. MINI FLOUR MILL
908. MINI SUGAR PLANT
909. MISRI (PEARL SUGAR CANDIES)
910. MODERN RICE MILL
911. MURABBA
912. MUSTARD OIL EXTRACTION & REFINING
913. MUTTON TALLOW
914. NAMKEEN INDUSTRY (BHUJIA, CHANA CHUR ETC.)
915. NAMKEEN & SWEETS
916. NON-BASMATI RICE FROM PADDY
917. OLEORESIN, ESSENTIAL OIL, DYES & POWDER OF SPICES
918. OLEORESIN EXTRACTION FROM DIPTERO-CARPUT TURMINATUS AND PINUS KHASYANA
919. OLEORESIN EXTRACTION FROM CHILLI
920. PAN MASALA AND POUCH

1059. BUFFALO HORN TIP, HOOF
1060. BANQUET HALL
1061. BUTTON
1062. CALCINED PETROLEUM (C.P) COKE
1063. CANVAS SHOES
1064. CANVAS SHOES, JUNGLE BOOTS
1065. CARBON BRUSH, BRUSH HOLDER & SLIP RING
1066. CEMENT SHEETS WITH COIR FIBRE & OTHER SEGMENTS
1067. CERAMIC TILES (GLAZED) BY DOUBLE FIRING/HEATING
1068. CHILDREN RECREATION CENTRE
1069. COAL BRIQUETTES
1070. COLD STORAGE & ICE
1071. COLD STORAGE FOR FRUITS AND VEGETABLES
1072. COMPRESSOR (HERMETIC) FOR AIR CONDITIONER
1073. COSTUME JEWELLERY/ IMITATION JEWELLERY
1074. DECORATIVE LAMINATED SHEET (SUNMICA)
1075. DIAMOND CUTTING & EXPORTS
1076. DRINKING STRAW FROM PROPYLENE
1077. ENGINEERING COLLEGE
1078. ENTERTAINMENT CLUB
1079. FASHION TECHNOLOGY INSTITUTE
1080. FAST FOOD PARLOUR
1081. FAST FOOD (INSTANT FOOD & FAST FOOD PARLOUR)
1082. FIRE EXTINGUISHERS (SODA ACID TYPE)
1083. FISH NET
1084. FLORICULTURE (CUT FLOWER ROSE) WITH GREEN HOUSE
1085. FLOOR COVERING SHEET
1086. FILM STUDIO (VIDEO)
1087. FLUSH DOOR, CHIP BOARD, WOOD WOOL & OTHER INSULATING BOARDS
1088. GAS DETECTORS OF L.P.G
1089. GEMS MANUFACTURING
1090. GLASS BOTTLE BY SCRAP
1092. GOAT & SHEEP FARMING
1093. GOLD ELECTROPLATING
1094. GOLD JEWELLERY (E.O.U)
1095. GOLD PLATED SILVER JEWELLERY & CUTLERY
1096. GRANITE SLAB AND TILES
1097. GREEN HOUSE
1098. HARD CHROMIUM PLATING
1099. HEALTH CLUB AND BEAUTY PARLOUR CUM HAIR SALOON WITH SONA BATH
1100. HEALTH CLUB CUM BEAUTY PARLOUR TRAININGINSTITUTE
1101. HORN TIP,HOOVE BUTTON
1102. HOSPITAL
1103. HOSPITAL (100 BEDS)
1104. HOSPITAL (200 BEDS)
1105. ICE MAKING PLANT
1106. IMITATION AND COSTUME
1107. JEWELLERY (NECKLACE, EARRINGS EAR TOP ETC.)
1108. INITMATE SCENT CHEMICALS FROM ALL TYPES OF FLAVOUR
1109. INVESTMENT CASTING
1110. JUTE, COIR, GLASS ROPE/ SUTLI
1111. JUTE TWINE
1112. L.P.G BOTTLING PLANT
1113. L.P.G REGULATOR (DOMESTIC PURPOSE)
1114. LAMINATED PARTICLE BOARD & HARD BOARD
1115. LAMINATED SAFETY AND TOUGHENED GLASS
1116. LEASING & HIRE PURCHASE
1117. LICHEN (CHARILA)
1118. MANILA ROPES
1119. MEDICAL COLLEGE
1120. MATCH UNIT FROM WAXED PAPER
1121. MEDIUM DENSITY FIBRE BOARD
1122. MELAMINE CROCKERY
1123. MINERAL WATER
1124. MINI CEMENT PLANT
1125. MIRROR SILVER, GOLDEN, PINK, BLACK & SMOKES
1126. MODERN ADVERTISING AGENCY WITH DTP & FILM STUDIO
1127. MOTEL/SMALL HOTEL
1128. MULTI COLOUR PRINTING
1129. MULTI STOREY COMMERCIAL COMPLEX ALONGWITH RESIDENTIALAND DELUX FLATS FOR FOREIGN TOURISTS & REVOLVING RESTAURENT AT THE TOP
1130. MULTIPLE LAMINATION INDUSTRY
1131. MUSHROOM GROWING AND PROCESSING (BY DEEP FREEZING METHOD)
1132. NEWS PAPER PRINTING
1133. NICKEL LINED INDUSTRIAL SCREEN
1134. OFFSET COLOUR PRINTING PRESS (SIX COLOUR)
1135. OFFSET PRINTING PRESS
1136. P.C.C ELECTRIC POLES
1137. PHOTOGRAPHIC DEVELOPER & FIXER
1138. PVC EXTRUSION PROFILE (DOOR & WINDOWS)
1139. POP-CORN
1140. PHOTO ETCHING OF S.S.
1141. PRE STRESSED CEMENT CONCRETE PIPES
1142. PILFER PROOF CAPS
1143. PILFER PROOF CAPS AND CROWN CAP
1144. POUCH MAKING & GRAVURE PRINTING (ROTO PRINTING)
1145. POULTRY & FISH FARMING (INTEGERATED UNIT)
1146. PRINTING OF TIN SHEETS
1147. READYMADE GARMENTS
1148. RESTAURANT
1149. ROSE PLANTATION AND ROSE OIL EXTRACTION
1150. ROTOGRAVURE PRINTING
1151. SAFETY BELTS
1152. SAFETY MATCHES
1153. SHOE LACES
1154. SILK COCOON CULTIVATION (GROWING OF SILK COCOON WARM)
1155. SILK SCREEN PRINTING FORMULATIONS FOR PLASTIC, PAPER & CLOTH
1156. SPIKENARD (JATAMANSI)
1157. STENCIL COATING SOLUTION
1158. SUGAR CANDY (MISRI)
1159. SUGAR CANE PLANTATION
1160. SUGAR CANE JUICE PRESERVATION
1161. SURAT ZARI
1162. SYNTHETIC SHOES & SOLES
1163. TEA PACKAGING INDUSTRY
1164. TENNIS BALLS
1165. THREE STAR HOTEL
1166. TRAVELLING AGENCY
1167. TRAYS, TROLLEYS FOR HOSPITAL WITH SCRATCHLESS COATING
1168. WAX EXTRACTS (TANNING POWDER)
1169. WIRE ROPE SLINGS
1170. WOOD WOOL SLAB
1171. WOODEN CANE FURNITURE WITH EXPORT POTENTIAL
1172. WOODEN FURNITURE
1173. WOODEN PANEL INCLUDING KILN SEASONING
1174. WOODEN FURNITURE
1175. WATCH CASE BUFFING
1176. WATCH DIAL
1177. WRIST WATCHES
1178. WATCHES (ELECTRONIC)
1179. ZEDOARY (KACHUR)

EDIBLE OILS, ESSENTIAL OILS LURICATIING OILS GREASES VEGETABLE OILS, WAXES CAMPHOR, PERFUMES & PERFUMERY COMPOUNDS AND REFINED OILS ETC

1180. AROMATIC PERFUMERY COMPOUND
1181. AEROSOL
1182. AGARBATTI PERFUMERY COMPOUND
1183. BEES WAX MANUFACTURE
1184. CAMPHOR
1185. CARDANOL FROM CASHEW NUT SHELL LIQUID
1186. CASTOR OIL
1187. CASTOR OIL DERIVATIVE OLEORESINS
1188. CHILLI OIL
1189. CITRONELLA OILS
1190. CLOVE OIL
1191. CONCENTRATE OF ROSE JASMINE & LILY ETC.
1192. COLOURED FLAME CANDLE

1193. CANDLES (SEMI-AUTOMATIC)
1194. CORN OIL (MAIZE OIL)
1195. DEHYDRATED CASTOR OIL
1196. EUGENOL FROM CINNAMON LEAF OIL
1197. EXTRACTION OF ESSENTIAL OIL (CARDAMON, JEERA, AJOWAN, GINGER OILS ETC. & PACKAGING OF GROUND SPICES)
1198. EXTRACTION OF JASMINE ESSENCE
1199. EXTRACTION OF ESSENTIAL OILS BY SUPER CRITICAL FLUID METHOD FROM FLOWERS, HERBS & SPICES
1200. EUCALYPTUS OIL
1201. EXTRACTION OF OIL FROM OIL SEED EXPANDEREXTRUSION TECHNOLOGY)
1202. FAT LIQUOR SULPHATED OIL
1203. FLAVOURS FOR FOOD
1204. GARLIC OIL & POWDER
1205. GINGER OIL, SANDALWOOD OIL AND NAGARMOTHA OIL
1206. GINGER OIL
1207. GINGER OIL & GINGER DUST
1208. INTEGERATED WAX COMPLEX
1209. IONONE FROM LEMON GRASS OIL
1210. JASMINE & LILLY FLOWER OIL
1211. LEMON GRASS OIL
1212. LIQUID PARAFFIN
1213. LUBE OIL & GREASE
1214. LUBRICATING OIL
1215. MENTHOL CRYSTALS
1216. MENTHOL OIL & CRYSTAL
1217. MICRO CRYSTALLINE WAX
1218. MUSTARD OIL (EDIBLE OIL)
1219. OIL FROM ARTEMISIA HERBS
1220. PALM OIL CRUSHING UNIT
1221. PAN MASALA
1222. PARAFFIN WAX
1223. PARAFFIN WAX FROM SLACK WAX
1224. REFINED OIL-SUN FLOWER OIL, GROUNDNUT OIL, STAFF FLOWER OIL & COTTON SEED OIL
1225. REFINED VEGETABLE OIL
1226. RECLAMATION OF USED ENGINE OIL
1227. RICE BRAN OIL (R.B.O)
1228. ROSE OIL EXTRACTION
1229. SMOKE LESS CANDLE
1230. SPICE OIL & OLEORESINS
1231. SOLVENT EXTRACTION PLANT (OIL CAKE BASED)
1232. SYNTHETIC ALMOND OIL
1233. SYNTHETIC TALLOW
1234. SYNTHETIC GHEE
1235. VEGETABLE OIL EXTRACTION & REFINING
1236. WADDING OIL (100%) FOR WADDING OF COTTON HOSIERY CLOTH IN DYEING PROCESS
1237. WAX EMULSION FOR TEXTILE
1238. WAX FLOOR POLISH

PAINT, ENAMEL, SOLVENTS, THINNERS, INKS & VARNISH

1239. ACRYLIC EMULSION PAINTS
1240. ALUMINIUM PAINT
1241. AUTOMOBILE PAINTS
1242. BALL POINT PEN REFILL INK
1243. BITUMINIOUS ROAD EMULSION
1244. BITUMEN
1245. BITUMINIOUS FELTS FOR WATER & DAMP PROOFING
1246. BITUMINIOUS ROAD EMULSION RAPID MEDIUM & SLOW SETTING
1247. BUFFING & POLISHING
1248. CEMENT PAINT FOR WHITE & GREY CEMENT

1249. DISPERSANT
1250. DRY DISTEMPER
1251. DRY DISTEMPER & CEMENT PAINT
1252. DUPLICATING INK BLACK FOR GESTNER DUPLICATOR
1255. EMULSION PAINTS (WATER BASED)
1256. HAMMERTONE PAINT
1257. INSULATING VARNISH & WIRE ENAMEL
1258. IRON OXIDE PIGMENTS
1259. INSULATING VARNISH (POLY VINYL BUTYRAL BASED, FFC GRADE)
1260. LIME COLOUR (CEMENT COLOUR)
1261. SYNTHETIC RED OXIDE FOR FLOORINGS
1262. SOLVENT & THINNERS
1263. MARKING INKS (WATER PROOF)
1264. METAL NAPHTHANATE (AS DRIER FOR PAINTS)
1265. N.C.PUTTY
1266. OFFSET PRINTING INK
1267. OIL BOUND DISTEMPER PAINT
1268. PAINT BRUSHES
1269. PAINT REMOVERS
1270. PAINT INDUSTRY
1271. PAINT & VARNISH
1272. PICTURE VARNISH
1273. POWDER COATING PAINT
1274. PRINTING INKS (OFFSET, FLEXO & ROTO GRAVURE)
1275. PRIMER PAINT & ENAMEL PAINT
1276. PUTTY & WATER PROOFING PAINT
1277. PRINTING INKS (FLEXO-GRAPHIC INK)
1278. PUTTY (METAL CASEMENT)
1279. RED OXIDE PRIMER (ANTI CORROSIVE)
1280. REFRACTORY PAINT (GRAPHITE BASED)
1281. SCREEN PRINTING INKS
1282. SILK SCREEN PRINTING INK FORMULATION FOR PLASTIC, PAPER, CLOTH
1283. STAMP & PAD INK
1284. STOVING PAINT
1285. SPIRIT SOLUBLE MALEIC RESIN
1286. TEXTURE PAINT
1287. THINNERS AND ITS ALLIED PRODUCTS
1288. TONER INK
1289. VARNISH THINNER (SOLVENT)
1290. VACUUM METALLIZING LACQUERS
1291. WOOD PRIMER

PHARMACEUTICAL, DRUGS, AYURVEDIC/HERBAL COSMETICS & MEDICINES, HOMOEOPATHIC MEDICINES, DISPOSABLE SYRINGE, DENTAL COLLEGE & FINE CHEMICALS ETC.

1292. AROMATIC PILLS
1293. ASPIRIN
1294. AYURVEDIC PAIN BALM OINTMENTS
1295. AYURVEDIC CHURAN AND TABLETS
1296. AYURVEDIC TABLETS (HAJMOLA TYPE)
1297. AYURVEDIC/HERBAL PHARMACY
1298. AYURVEDIC SHERBATS
1299. AYURVEDIC PRODUCTS
1300. BULK DRUGS (E.O.U)
1301. BLOOD BAGS
1302. CALCIUM GLUCONATE
1303. CAPSULE, TABLET & INJECTION WITH MODERN INSTRUMENTS
1304. CASHEW FENI
1305. CHLOROQUINONE PHOSPHATE (BULK DRUGS)
1306. CLINICAL THERMOMETER
1307. DENTAL CLINIC

1308. DENTAL COLLEGE
1309. DENTAL GRADE EUGENOL
1310. DEXTROSE MONOHYDRATE, LIQUID GLUCOSE
1311. DEHYDRATED ONION & ONION POWDER
1312. DEXTROSE POWDER (ANHYDROUS FROM STARCH)
1314. DEXTROSE SALINE SOLUTION
1315. DISTILLERY (I.M.F.L)
1316. DISPOSABLE NEEDLES FOR SYRINGES
1317. DISPRIN
1318. DISTILLED WATER
1319. EMPTY HARD GELATINE CAPSULES
1320. FILLING & PACKING OF CAPSULES
1321. GLUCOSE - D - POWDER
1322. GLYCERINE
1323. HERBAL COSMETICS
1324. HERBAL SHAMPOO
1325. HERBAL HAIR OILS (AYURVEDIC)
1326. HOMOE & BIO-MEDICINES WITH MOTHER TINCTURE
1327. HOMOEPATHIC MEDICINES
1328. HYPODERMIC NEEDLES
1329. I.V. FLUIDS
1330. IBUPROFEN
1331. INFUSION & TRANSFUSION SETS (I.V. SET)
1332. INJECTABLE FOR PHARMACEUTICALS
1333. INJECTION AMPOULES PACKAGING BOX
1334. INTEGERATED SURGICAL COTTON
1335. ICE MAKING PLANT
1336. ICE & COLD STORAGE
1337. LACTOSE & BY PRODUCTS PROCESSING FROM MILK
1338. LICHEN (JATAMANSI CHARILA)
1339. LIQUID GLUCOSE AND ITS BY-PRODUCTS
1340. L-LYSINE MONOHYDRO CHLORIDE
1341. LIQUID GLUCOSE FROM POTATOES
1342. MEDICAL COLLEGE
1343. NICOTINE FROM TOBACCO WASTE
1344. OINTMENT-AYURVEDIC (YELLOW & WHITE)
1345. PHARMACEUTICAL AND FOOD GRADE GELATINE
1346. PHARMACEUTICAL INDUSTRY (TABLETS, CAPSULES, LIQUID, GEL, OINTMENT POWDER INJECTABLE)
1347. PHARMACEUTICAL UNIT (EOU) WITH FORMULA TIONS, INJECTABLES, ETC. PYRIDINE & DERIVATIVES
1348. SALT (IODIZED SALT)
1349. SALINE & INJECTION WATER
1350. SALINE WATER & DEXTROSE SOLUTION (I.V.FLUID IN PLASTIC BOTTLES)
1351. SORBITOL
1352. STARCH (MAIZE)
1353. SURGICAL ADHESIVE PLASTER
1354. SURGICAL BANDAGES
1355. SURGICAL GLOVES
1357. SURGICAL COTTON
1358. SURGICAL COTTON AND BANDAGE
1359. SYNTHETIC CAMPHOR POWDER
1360. TABLETS & CAPSULES
1361. TISSUE CULTURE
1362. TINCTURE FROM RECTIFIED SPIRIT
1363. TRIMETHOPIME
1364. VETERENARY MEDICINES (ONLY FORMULATIONS)
1365. VITAMIN 'C', SORBITOL' ANHYDROUS DEXTROSE, STARCH

PULP, PAPER, STRAW/GREY BOARD, KRAFT PAPER, PACKAGING, PAPER CARRY BAGE, PAPER FROM AGRO WASTE & STATIONERY ETC.

1366. AMMONIA PAPER
1367. AUTOMATIC BOOK BINDING
1368. ADHESIVE (FEVICOL TYPE)
1369. ALL PIN & GEM CLIPS
1370. CARBON PAPER
1371. CARD BOARD
1372. CARBON LESS PAPER
1373. CELLPHANE PAPER
1374. COMPUTER FORMS & SECURITY PRINTING PRESS
1375. CORRUGATED BOARD & BOX (PRINTED & LAMINATED)
1376. CORRUGATED BOARD AND BOXES FROM FROM CARD BOARDS
1377. CORRUGATED CARTONS FROM PLAIN PAPERS
1378. CORRUGATRED PACKING & MATERIAL (BULB & TUBES PACKING)
1379. DESK TOP PUBLISHING
1380. DEFOAMING AGENT FOR PAPER PLANT
1381. DRINKING STRAW PAPER
1382. D.T.P CUM OFFSET PRESS
1383. EGG TRAYS
1384. EXERCISE NOTE BOOK, REGISTER AND PAD
1385. FLEXOGRAPHIC INK
1386. GREETING CARD BY OFFSET PRESS
1387. HAND MADE PAPER FILTER PAPER
1388. HARD BOARD
1389. INJECTION AMPOULES PACKAGING BOXES
1390. INSULATIING PAPER
1391. KRAFT PAPER
1392. KRAFT PAPER FROM BAGASSE
1393. LAMINATED PACKAGING PAPER WITH PRINTING
1394. LAMINATION & COATING ON PAPER
1395. M.G. PAPER FROM WASTE PAPER
1396. MILL PAPER FROM WASTE PAPER
1397. MILL BOARD FROM RICE & WHEAT STRAWS
1398. MILL BOARD FROM WASTE PAPER
1399. MINI PAPER PLANT FROM SISAL
1400. MINI PAPER PLANT
1401. MULTI WALL PAPER SACKS
1402. NEWS PAPER FOR CHILDREN
1403. NEWS PRINT PAPER FROM RICE STRAW BAGASSE
1404. NEWS PAPER CHILDRENS
1405. NEWS PRINT PAPER
1406. OFFSET AND TREADLE TYPE PRINTING PRESS
1407. MILL BOARD BASED ON RICE STRAW
1408. PAPER AND BOARD FROM STRAW
1409. PAPER & PAPER PRODUCTS
1410. PAPER ENVELOPES
1411. PAPER CARRY BAGS
1412. PAPER BOARD CARTON
1413. PAPER CONES FOR LOUD SPEAKERS
1414. PAPER FROM AKRA
1415. PAPER FROM BAGASSE WITH CORRUGATED BOARD & BOXES
1416. PAPER FROM BAMBOO
1417. PAPER GLASSES FOR BEVERAGES
1418. PAPER FROM RICE HUSK & WHEAT HUSK
1419. PAPER FROM TREE BARK, EUCALYPRUS WOOD
1420. PAPER PRODUCTS
1421. PAPER PLANT (WHITE WRITING & NEWS PAPER FOR PULP & WASTE PAPER)
1422. PAPER PLATES, PAPER GLASS
1423. PAPER CONES & TUBES
1425. PAPER PLANT WITH DTP & PRINTING & PUBLISHING UNIT
1426. PAPER BASED PHENOLIC SHEET
1427. PAPER CUP FOR ICE CREAM
1428. PAPER TUBES SPIRAL WINDING COMPOSIT CONTAINER
1429. PAPER LABLE FOR BEER BOTTLES
1430. PARTICLE BOARD & BLACK BOARD WITH SANDING & LAMINATION OF PARTICLE BOARD
1431. PARTICLE BOARD FROM RICE HUSK
1432. POUCH FILLING & MAKING FOR TOMATO SAUCE
1433. POUCH MAKING &

GRAVURE PRINTING
1434. PROCESSING OF PAPER FOR FEEDING IN COMPUTER
1435. PULP FROM BAMBOO & WOOD
1436. PAPER FILES
1437. PLAYING CARDS
1438. ROSIN SIZING AGENT (FOR PAPER PLANT)
1439. SAND PAPER
1440. SANITRY NAPKINS
1441. SILICON COATED PAPER
1442. STENCIL PAPER
1443. STRAW BOARD AND GREY BOARD
1444. STRAW BOARD & MILL BOARD
1445. STRAW BOARD AND PAPER BOARD
1446. TISSUE PAPER FACIAL
1447. TISSUE MOIST TOILETERY CLEANSING TISSUE AND RELATED PRODUCTS
1448. TISSUE PAPER ROLLS
1449. TETRA PACK FOR MILK PACKAGING, GHEE & OTHER LIQUIDS
1450. TOILET PAPER ROLLS
1451. TOILET PAPER & NAPKINS
1452. WAX COATED PRINTED PAPER
1453. WET FACE FRESHNER TISSUE
1454. WHITE WRITING & PRINTING PAPER
1455. WRITING & PRINTING PAPER (PAPER MILLS)

PLASTIC, B.O.P.P, ACRYLIC, DISPOSABLE PLASTIC PRODUCTS, PET PRODUCTS, P.V.C, H.D.P.E, P.P, L.D.P.E., P.U, A.B.S, THERMOFOARMING, MASTER BATCHES, & POLYMER AND RUBBER PRODUCTS, TYRE, TUBE, ADHESIVE, SHEET, COIR & MANY OTHERS

1456. ABS GRANULES FROM ABS SCRAPS FROM OLD T.V. CABINETS, WHITE GOODS ETC.
1457. ACRYLIC BEADS
1458. ACRYLIC COPOLYMER EMULSION
1459. ACRYLIC LATEX
1460. ACRYLIC SHEET
1461. ACRYLIC SHEET & MOULDED PRODUCTS
1462. ACRYLIC TEETH
1463. AUTO TUBES
1464. AUTO FLAPS FOR TRUCKS & BUSES
1465. AUTO TYRES & TUBES
1466. BABY BOTTLES (PLASTIC) WITH WHITESILICON RUBBER NIPPLES
1467. B.O.P.P. FILM
1468. B.O.P.P. PRESSURE SENSITIVE SELF ADHESIVE TAPE
1469. BABY NIPPLE (SILICON)
1470. BABY NIPPLE (BIG SIZE)
1471. BALLOON PLASTIC ADVERTISING
1472. BLISTER FILM PVC
1473. BLISTER PACKAGING & POUCH PAKAGING
1474. BLOW MOULDING PLASTIC CONTAINER
1475. COATING ON METALIZED POLYESTER FILM/METALISED PAPER/ ALIMINIUM FOIL
1476. COATING ON PLASTIC (ELECTROLYSIS) & GLASS
1477. COIR FOAM (RUBBERISED)
1478. COLOUR COATING ON PLASTICS
1479. COLOUR MASTER BATCHES FOR VARIOUS PLASTICS
1480. CYCLE TYRES AND TUBES
1481. DISPOSABLE PLASTIC CUPS GLASSES, ETC.
1482. DISPOSABLE PLASTIC SYRINGES & NEEDLES
1483. DISPOSABLE PLASTIC SYRINGES
1484. DOUGH MOULDING COMPOUND (D.M.C)
1485. EPOXY RESIN
1486. EXPANDED POLYESTRENE MOULDING (THERMOCOLE)
1487. F.R.P AUTO,SCOOTER ROOFS & CEILINGS
1488. F.R.P PRODUCTS (HELMET, WASHBASIN SHEETS, ROOFING SHEETS)
1489. FIBRE REINFORCED PLASTIC (HIGH PRESSURE MOULDING WITH SMC BMC AND DMC)
1490. FIELD RUBBER CONVERTED TO THE 60% LATEX RUBBER
1491. FLEXIBLE P.U. FOAM
1492. FORMALDEHYDE CROCKERY & OTHER ITEMS
1493. FORMALDEHYDE RESIN (UREA, PHENOL,MELEMINE)
1494. GASKET SHEET
1495. GUM BOTTLE (PVC)
1496. GLASS BEADS
1497. HDPE COATED PAPER SACK
1498. H.D.P.E. BAGS
1499. H.D.P.E. CONTAINERS (BLOW MOULDING)
1500. H.D.P.E. CONTAINER, POLY JARS BY INJECTION MOULDING (FOOD GRADE)
1501. H.D.P.E. JERRY CANS
1502. HDPE MANUFACTURING FROM ETHYLALCOHOL
1503. H.D.P.E PIPE AND FITTINGS
1504. H.D.P.E. PIPES
1505. H.D.P.E PRINTED BAGS
1506. H.D.P.E TWINES AND ROPES
1507. H.D.P.E. & L.D.P.E PIPES AND FITTINGS
1508. H.D.P.E/PP BOX STRAPPING
1509. H.D.P.E/PP WOVEN SACKS USING PLAIN LOOMS
1510. HOLOGRAM STICKERS-3D
1511. H.M BAG PLANT WITH PRINTING UNIT
1512. HAWAI CHAPPALS (RUBBER)
1513. I.V PLASTIC BOTTLE
1514. ICE CREAM CUP (PLASTIC)
1515. INJECTION MOULDED AUTO COMPONENTS
1516. INJECTION & BLOW MOULDED PLASTIC PRODUCTS
1517. INJECTION MOULDED PLASTIC PRODUCTS
1518. INTEGERATED COMPLEX ESTER'S & ALLIED PRODUCTS (D.O.P,D.B.P, & ETHYL ACETATE, BUYTL ACETATE, WIRE ENAMELS, JELLY CABLE COMPOUND)
1519. L.D.P.E. (LOW DENSITY POLY ETHYLENE) GRANULES FROM VIRGIN (L.D.P.E. RESIN)
1520. INTEGERATED SURGICAL RUBBER GOODS INDUSTRY
1521. INJECTION MOULDED PLASTIC BALLS
1522. L.D.P.E FROM ETHYL ALCOHOL
1523. LDPE MOULDED PRODUCTS
1524. LAMINATION OF COEXTRUSION MULTILAYER FILM IN ROLL FORM
1525. LATEX RUBBER
1526. LATEX RUBBER CONDOM
1527. MASTER BATCHES (COLOURED, P.V.C, L.D.P.E, H.D.P.E, ETC.)
1528. MELAMINE FORMALHYDE RESIN
1529. MOULDED LUGGAGE
1530. MULTI-LAYER (3 LAYER BAGS)
1531. MULTI-LAYER (3 LAYER) FILM WITH LAMINATION & PRINTING
1532. OIL SEAL
1533. PET BOTTLE/CONTAINERS
1534. PET BOTTLES FROM PRE FORM
1535. PET BOTTLE & MINERAL WATER
1536. PET PRE-FORM FROM PET RESIN
1537. PET PRE-FORM CUM PET BOTTLES
1538. PET PRE-FORM PET BOTTLES CUM MINERAL WATERS
1539. POLY CARBONATE RESIN
1540. PTFE COMPONENTS
1541. PU/PVC SOLE FOR SPORT SHOE BY IMPORTED M/C.
1542. PVC BATTERY SEPARATOR
1543. P.V.C COMPOUNDS (FRESH)
1544. P.V.C COMPOUNDS (SCRAP)
1545. P.V.C ELECTRICAL INSULATING TAPE
1546. P.V.C. EXTRUSION PROFILES
1547. P.V.C FITTINGS
1548. P.V.C FLEXIBLE FUSIBLE POWDER HEAT FUSIBLE POWDER
1549. P.V.C GRANULES (FOR

INSULATION & SHEETS GRADES)
1550. P.V.C GRANULES FROM PVC SCRAPS (WITH POLLUTION CONTROL)
1551. P.V.C HOSES
1552. P.V.C LEATHER CLOTH
1553. P.V.C FLEXIBLE PIPES
1554. P.V.C PIPES AND FITTINGS
1555. POLYTHENE BAGS (PRINTED)
1556. PVC PLASTICS FILM SHEET SOFT/RIGID
1557. PVC RESIN AND COMPOUND
1558. PVC RULAR
1559. PVC STABLIZERS (SINGLE PACK SYSTEM)
1560. PVC WIRE AND CABLES
1561. PAPER BASED PHENOLIC SHEET FOR ELECTRICAL
1562. PHENOL FORMALDEHYDE RESIN
1563. PHENOLIC RESIN
1564. PLASTIC BEADS FROM PLASTIC SCRAPS
1565. PLASTIC BUTTONS
1566. PLASTIC CANS
1567. PLASTIC COLLAPSIBLE TUBE
1568. PLASTIC CORRUGATED SHEET & BOXES
1569. PLASTIC FILM AND SHEETS WITH PRINTING FLEXO & ROTO/LDPE/HDPE/PP/HM/PVC
1570. PLASTIC FILTER MASTER BATCH & OTHER MASTER BATCHES FOR VARIOUS PLASTICS
1571. PLASTIC JERRY CANS
1572. PLASTIC GRANULES OR POWDER FROM PLASTIC SCRAP
1573. PLASTIC INJECTION MOULDED T.V. CABINETS
1574. PLASTIC ITEMS MANUFAC TURE FROM POWDER MELAMINE
1575. PLASTIC GOODS
1576. PLASTIC PIPES & TARPAULINES
1577. PLASTIC SHEET FROM SCRAP
1578. PLASTIC PLANT (BLOW MOULDING & INJECTION MOULDING)
1579. PLASTIC PRODUCTS (GOLD, SILVER, NICKEL)
1580. PLASTIC TOYS
1581. POLYESTER BEADING
1582. POLYESTER FILM
1583. POLYTHENE BAGS & AUTOMATIC PRINTING
1584. POLYTHENE PRINTED BAGS
1585. POLYURETHANE FOAM AND ITS PRODUCTS
1586. PROPYLENE FILM (PRINTED) & BAG MANUFACTURING
1587. PLASTIC MATS
1588. RAINBOW COLOUR ON PVC FILM & SHEET
1589. RED MUD PVC PIPES AND FITTINGS
1590. RE-RUBBERISED OF SOLID TYPE
1591. RESIN COATED SAND REXINE
1592. REXINE CLOTH & ALLIED PRODUCTS
1593. RUBBER ADHESIVE
1594. RUBBER AUTO PARTS
1595. RUBBER BELTING
1596. RUBBER MOULDING UNIT INCLUDING LINING RUBBER SHEETING
1597. RUBBER RECLAIMING
1598. RUBBER ROLLERS FOR TEXTILE MILLS & PAPER INDUSTRIES
1599. RUBBER & PLASTIC SHEETS MATS & FLAPS
1600. RUBBER SHEET AND ALLIED HOSPITAL RUBBER GOODS
1601. RUBBERIZED PVC GASKET
1602. RUBBERISED COIR
1603. RUBBER COMPOUND FOR AUTOMOBILES
1604. SAFETY BELTS
1605. SILVER AND GOLD PLATING ON PVC AND NYLON-6
1606. SILICONE RUBBER NIPPLES/ TEATS
1607. SPECTACLE FRAMES (PLASTIC)
1608. SPUNGE RUBBER
1609. SURGICAL EXAMINATION GLOVES
1610. SYNTHETIC PEARL COATING ON POLYSTYRENE BEADS
1611. SYNTHETIC RUBBER ADHESIVE
1612. TEFLON MANUFACTURING
1613. TEFLON TAPE
1614. TEFLON TAPES & CABLES
1615. THERMOCOLE SHEET AND MOULDED PRODUCTS EXPANDED POLYESTERENE EXTRUSION PROFILES
1616. THERMOFORMED PACKAGING (BLISTER PACKAGING & POUCH PACKAGING)
1617. THERMOPLASTIC POLYURETHANE
1618. THERMOFORMED CUPS, PLATES & GLASS WITH HIPS SHEET
1619. THERMOCOLE
1620. THERMOCOLE BASED DISPOSABLE GLASS, CUPS & PLATES
1621. TOOTH BRUSHES
1622. TOY BALLOON, DECORA TIVE & INDUSTRIAL BALLOONS
1623. TREAD RUBBER
1624. TYRE RETREADING (HOT)
1625. TYRE RETREADING BY COLD PROCESS
1626. TYRE TUBES & FLAPS
1627. TYRE & TUBES
1628. UNSATURATED POLYESTER FOR REXINE
1629. V-BELT AND FAN BELT
1630. VINYL ASBESTOS AND PVC WALL PAPER
1631. VITON (FLUORO ELASTOMER)

SOAP, COSMETICS & PERFUMS

1632. ACID SLURRY, SYNTHETIC DETERGENT POWDER
1632. ACID SLURRY
1633. AGARBATTI SYNTHETIC, PERFUMERY COMPOUND
1634. AFTER SHAVE LOTION
1635. ANTISEPTIC CREAM
1636. BETA IONONE
1637. BLEACHING POWDER
1638. BLUE DETERGENT POWDER
1639. CLEANING POWDER (VIMTYPE)
1640. COLD CREAM
1641. COLOURED FLAME & PERFUMED CANDLES (RED, BLUE, GREEN FLAME)
1642. COSMETIC INDUSTRY (MODERN)
1643. COSMETIC INDUSTRY (SHAMPOO, SPRAY PERFUME, TALCUM POWDER
1644. DETERGENT POWDER (ARIEL TYPE)
1645. DETERGENT POWDER (NIRMA TYPE) FULLY AUTOMATIC PLANT
1646. DETERGENT WASHING POWDER
1647. FISH OIL SOAP
1648. GLYCERINE TRANSPARENT SOAP
1649. HAIR REMOVING CREAM
1650. HERBAL COSMETICS
1651. HERBAL SHAMPO & CREAM
1652. HERBAL/AYURVEDIC COSMETICS
1653. INCENSE POWDER, INCENSE STICKS & INCENSE CAKE
1654. OPTICAL WHITENERS
1655. ROSE OIL EXTRACTION
1656. SHAMPOOS (COCONUT OIL BASED COLD PROCESS)
1657. SHAVING CREAM
1658. SINDUR (KUMKUM)
1659. SOAP COATED PAPER
1660. SPRAY DRIED DETERGENT POWDER
1661. STAIN REMOVER
1662. TALCUM POWDER (FACE & TOILET POWDER)
1663. TOILET AND HERBAL SOAP
1664. TOOTH PASTE & POWDER
1665. WASHING DETERGENT POWDER AND WASHING SOAP
1666. WASHING POWDER LIQUID DETERGENTS, LOTION & SHAMPOO

TEXTILE INDUSTRIES, READYMADE GARMENTS, COTTON, DYEING, BLEACHING, CLOTH, HOSIERY, POWER LOOM, HAND LOOM, WOOLLEN, SILK, SOCKS, SURGICAL COTTON & MANY OTHERS

1667. ANGORA RABBIT WOOL
1668. BUCKRAM
1669. CANVAS SHOES, JUNGLE BOOT, BOOT RUBBER KNEES & BOOT COMBAT
1670. CARPET FROM COTTON WASTE
1671. CERAMIC THREAD GUIDE
1672. COTTON BUDS/SWABS
1673. COTTON FROM WASTE YARN
1674. COTTON ROLLS
1675. COTTON SPIDERS FOR LOUD SPEAKERS
1676. DENIM CLOTH
1677. DENIM CLOTH (INTEGERATED UNIT WITH BLEACHING, DYEING AND PRINTING)
1678. DISPERSENT FOR TEXTILE
1679. DYEING & BLEACHING
1680. DYEING OF HANK YARN
1681. EMULSIFIER FOR WOOL BATCHING OIL
1682. EMBROIDERY ON FABRICS
1683. GARMENT DYEING, WASHING & STITCHING (JEANS, JACKETS, SKIRTS & SHIRTS)
1684. GOVES KNITTING
1685. GUNNY BAGS
1687. HDPE WOVEN SACKS
1688. HDPE TARPAULINS USING PLAIN LOOM WITH LAMINATION
1689. HDPE/PP WOVEN SACKS USING CIRCULAR LOOMS
1690. HOSIERY CLOTH (COTTON) PROCESSING (BLEACHING, DYEING, FINISHING OF CLOTH)
1691. HOSIERY INDUSTRY
1692. HOSIERY MERCERISING
1693. HOSIERY PRODUCTS LIKE VEST, BRIEF, T-SHIRTS & SOCKS
1694. JACQUARD FABRICS
1695. JUTE COIR, GRASS ROPE/ SUTLI MAKING
1696. JUTE FELT
1697. JUTE TWINES
1698. KNITTED FABRICS
1699. LAMINATED JUTE BAGS
1700. LAMINATION OF HDPE WOVEN CLOTH (JUTE,COTTON, PAPER)
1701. NYLON YARN CRIMPING, DOUBLING AND BLEACHING
1702. PIGMENT BINDER FOR TEXTILE PRINTING
1704. POLYESTER RESIN FOR WIRE ENAMEL
1705. POLYESTER RESIN
1706. POLYESTER YARN FROM WASTE POLYESTER ZIP FASTENERS
1707. POWER LOOM
1708. READYMADE GARMENTS & HOSIERY
1709. READYMADE GARMENTS MERCHANDISE
1710. READYMADE GARMENTS & COVERS
1711. READYMADE GARMENTS & EMBROIDERY OF GOWNS, SHIRTS, BLOUSES, T-SHIRTS ETC. (ONLY LADIES)
1712. READYMADE SALWAR SUIT
1713. RECOVERY OF NYLON FROM NYLON WASTE
1714. ROTARY PRINTING AND DYEING ON COTTON, SYNTHETIC TEXTILE
1715. SANITARY NAPKINS
1716. SCREEN PRINTING ON COTTON CLOTH
1717. SEWING THREAD REELS & BALLS MAKING INDUSTRIES
1718. SCREEN PRINTING ON COTTON, POLYESTER & ACRYLIC
1719. SHAWLS (WOOLLEN)
1720. SHOE LACES
1721. SILK FABRICS ON HANDLOOM
1722. SOCKS KNITTING
1723. SPINNING, DOUBLING DYEING MERCERISING & BLEACHING OF COTTON YARN
1724. SPINNING & CARDING OF WOOL INTO YARNS
1725. STARCH BOOK BINDING CLOTH
1726. SURAT JARI
1727. SURGICAL COTTON & BANDAGE
1728. SYNTHETIC TEXTILE INDUSTRY(SUITING, SHIRTING, SAREES) TERRY CLOTH
1729. T-SHIRTS
1730. TOWELS, BED SHEET COVERS
1731. TERRY TOWEL
1732. TERRY FABRICS WEAVING UNIT
1733. TEXTILE AUXILLIARIES & CHEMICALS
1734. TEXTILE BLEACHING, DYEING & FINISHING & PRINTING OF COTTON FABRICS
1735. TEXTILE (HOSIERY)
1736. TEXTILE MILL
1737. TEXTILE DYEING & PRINTING
1738. TEXTILE PRINTING (JOB WORK)
1739. TEXTILE PIGMENT PRINTING BINDER
1740. TOWEL (TERRY)
1741. VELVET CLOTH BY FLOCKING PROCESS
1742. VISCOSE STAPLE FIBRE
1743. WADDING OIL (100%) FOR WADDING OF COTTON HOSIERY CLOTH IN THE DYEING PROCESS
1744. WEAVING OF DASUTI CLOTH WITH PRINTING, DYEING, EMBROIDERY & FINISHING
1745. WASHING OF JEANS & OTHER GARMENTS
1746. WORSTED WOOLLEN YARN CLOTH
1747. ZARI GLITTER SALMA SITARA OF PLASTIC FILM

INFOTECH/IT, HOSPITALITY, HOSPITAL, COLLEGE, SCHOOL, MEDICAL, ENTERTAINMENT CLUB, WARE HOUSING & REAL ESTATE, PROJECTS

1748. AMUSEMENT PARK
1749. AMUSEMENT PARK CUM WATER PARK
1750. BANQUET HALL
1751. CALL CENTER (DOMESTIC)
1752. CALL CENTER (INTERNATIONAL)
1753. CHILDREN RECREATION CENTRE
1754. COLD STORAGE
1755. COMMUNITY HALL
1756. COMPUTER EDUCATION INSTITUTE
1757. COMPUTER SOFTWARE
1758. COLLEGE
1759. CYBER CAFE
1760. DENTAL CLINIC
1761. DENTAL COLLEGE
1762. DIAGONOSTIC CENTRE
1763. E-COMMERCE/BUSINESS
1764. E-SCHOOL (Rs. 5000/-)
1765. ENGINEERING COLLEGE
1766. ENTERTAINMENT CLUB
1767. ENTERTAINMENT CLUB, HOLIDAY RESORT, 4 STAR HOTEL, AMUSEMENT PARK CUM WATER PARK, MUSHROOM & ITS PRODUCTS, FISH FARMING, LAKE FOR BOATING, DEER PARK
1768. FASHION TECHNOLOGY INSTITUTE
1769. FAST FOOD PARLOUR
1770. FIVE STAR HOTEL
1771. FOOD PARLOUR
1772. FRANCHISE TRAINING PROGRAMME FOR IIT & ENGINEERING ENTRANCE EXAMS.
1773. GOLF COURSE
1774. HEALTH CLUB, BEAUTY PARLOUR
1775. HEALTH CLUB AND FITNESS CENTER
1776. HEALTH RESORTS
1777. HOLIDAY RESORTS
1778. HOLIDAY RESORT CUM

ENTERTAINMENT CLUB WITH 4 STAR HOTEL
1779. HOSPITALS
1780. ICE CREAM PARLOUR
1781. INTERNET SERVICE PROVIDER (I.S.P.)
1782. MEDICAL COLLEGE
1783. MEDICAL COLLEGE, HOSPITAL & RESEARCH INSTITUTE
1784. MEDICAL TRANSCRIPTION CENTRE
1785. MENTAL RETARDATION HOSPITAL & CEREBRAL PALSY
1786. MOTEL/SMALL HOTEL
1787. MULTISTOREY COMMERCIAL COMPLEX
1788. MULTISTOREY RESIDENTIAL COMPLEX
1789. NURSERY SCHOOL
1790. NATURE CARE CENTRE
1791. NURSING HOME
1792. ONLINE SHOPPING MALL (RS. 5000/- REPORT)
1793. PORTAL
1794. REHABILITATION CENTRE FOR AGED & NEEDY PERSONS
1795. RESIDENTIAL CUM COMMERCIAL COMPLEX
1796. RESTAURANT
1797. RESTAURANT WITH PUB
1798. SCHOOL (PRIMARY)
1799. SCHOOL (HIGHER SECONDARY)
1800. THREE STAR HOTEL
1801. TOURIST CLUB
1802. TRAINING INSTITUTE FOR MEDICAL TRANSCRIPTION
1803. VIDEO FILM STUDIO
1804. WARE HOUSE
1805. WEBSITE DESIGN & E-MAIL REGISTERING

AGRO BASED INDUSTRIES

1806. COAL BRIQUETTES FROM AGROWASTE
1807. FURFURALFROM RICEHULL
1808. MUSHROOM CULTIVATION & PROCESSING (BUTTON)
1809. MUSHROOM GROWING & PROCESSING WITH AIR CONDITIONING
1810. MUSHROOM CULTIVATION & PROCESSING UNIT DEHYDRATION & PACKAGING OF OYSTER & PADDY STRAW MUSHROOMS
1811. ORGANIC MANURE
1812. PAPAYA CULTIVATION
1813. PAPAYA & TOMATO CULTIVATION
1814. PROCESSING & UTILISATION OF COCONUT
1815. PROCESSING OF SHEEP HAIR TO PRODUCE WOOL

BAKERY, CONFECTIONERY & FOOD PRODUCTS

1816. AGROLACTOR SOYA MILK
1817. APPLE FRUIT JUICE WITH CANNING BOTTLING
1818. AYURVEDIC SHARBAT
1819. BAKERY UNIT (PASTRIES, BREAD, BUNS, CAKE, TOFFEE ETC.)
1820. BAKING POWDER
1821. BANANA & ITS BY PRODUCTS
1822. BANANA POWDER
1823. BANANA WAFERS
1824. BANANA CULTIVATION
1825. BEER INDUSTRY
1826. DEHULLING OF JAUN FOR BEER
1827. BEER & WINE
1828. BEER, ALCOHOL, IMFL
1829. BESEN PLANT
1830. BISCUIT PLANT
1831. BREAD & BISCUIT PLANT
1832. BOTTLING PLANT COUNTRY LIQUOR FROM RECTIFIED SPIRIT
1833. BRANDY
1834. BREAD RUSKS
1835. CANNED FRUITS & VEGETABLES
1836. CANNING & PRESERVATION OF MEAT
1837. CANNING & PRESERVATION OF VEGETABLES
1838. CANNING OF MANGO PULP & MANGO SLICES
1839. CARBONATED BEVERAGS
1840. CASHEW FENI
1841. CASHEW NUT (DRIED & FRIED)
1842. CATTLE BREEDING
1843. CATTLE BREEDING & DAIRY FARM TO PRODUCE MILK
1844. CATTLE FEED FROM TAPIOCA
1845. CHEWING GINGER & AMLOKI
1846. CHEWING GUM
1847. CHILLI SAUCE
1848. CHILLI POWDER
1849. CHOCOLATE
1850. CIDER PLANT
1851. COCOA POWDER
1852. COCOA BUTTER & COCOA POWDER
1853. COCONUT SHELL POWDER
1854. COCONUT WATER
1855. COCONUT SWEET (WATERY)
1856. COCONUT MILK POWDER (DEHYDRATED)
1857. COCONUT PRODUCTS & BY PRODUCTS (INTEGRATED PLANT)
1858. COLD DRINK
1859. CURRY POWDER
1860. DAIRY FOR MILK PROCESSING (GHEE, BUTTER & PANEER)
1861. DAIRY PRODUCTS
1862. DAIRY PRODUCTS MILK PACKAGING IN POUCH (GHEE, BUTTER, ETC.
1863. DAIRY FARM TO PRDUCE MILK WITH PACKAGING (COW)
1864. DAIRY FARM TO PRDUCE MILK WITH PACKAGING (BUFALLOE)
1865. DAIRY FARM & MILK PRODUCTS
1866. DAL MOTH, CHANACHUR & BHUJIYA
1867. DEHYDRATION OF FRUITS & VEGETABLE
1868. DESICCATED COCONUT POWDER FROM COCONUTS
1869. DEHYDRATION & CANNINGOF FRUITS & VEGETABLES
1870. DRY FRUIT ROASTING & PACKAGING
1871. DRYING OF RED CHILLIES, HALDI, DHANIYA, PEAS & GROUND NUT
1872. EGG POWDER
1873. FISH CANNING IN TIN & POUCHES
1874. FISH DEHYRATION (DRYING OF FISH)
1875. FISH MEAL
1876. FISH PROCESSING (BEAST FREEZING PROCESSES)
1877. FLAVOURS FOR FOOD INDUSTRIES
1878. FLOUR MILL (ROLLER)
1879. FROZEN MEAT
1880. FOOD DEHYDRATION (FRUITS & VEGETABLES)
1881. FRIED & ROASTED GROUND NUT, GRAMS, PEAR ETC.
1882. FRUIT JUICE MAKING & PACKAGING IN PLASTIC CONTAINER
1883. FRUIT JUICE IN TETRA PACK (DRINKS)
1884. FRUIT JUICE, SQUASHES, SAUCE & KETCHUP, JAM, JELLY, VINEGAR ETC.
1885. GARLIC FLAKES
1886. GARLIC POWDER
1887. GHEE & BUTTER
1888. GINGER (PULVERISED)
1889. GINGER GLAZING & PRESERVATION
1890. GINGER STORAGE
1891. GINGER PROCESSING
1892. GINGER OIL & GINGER DUST
1893. GINGER POWDER (DRY) & OLEORESIN
1894. GRAPE DEHYDRATION
1895. GRAPE CULTIVATION
1896. GRAPE JUICE
1897. HONEY PROCESSING & PACKAGING
1898. ICE CREAM & ICE CANDY
1899. ICE CUBE
1900. INVERT SUGAR
1901. IDLI MIX, DOSA MIX SAMBHAR MIX, VADA MIX, GULAB JAMUN MIX
1902. INSTANT COFFEE & INSTANT TEA

1903. INSTANT NOODLES
1904. INSTANT SOUPS
1905. IODIZED SALT FROM CRUDE SALT
1906. JAM CHUTNEY PICKLES & SQUASHES
1907. KATHA MANUFACTURING
1908. LECITHIN (SOYA BASED)
1909. LEMON & ITS PRODUCTS
1910. MACARONI MANUFACTURING
1911. MACARONI, SPAGHETTI, VERMICELLI & NOODLES
1912. MAIZE & ITS BY PRODUCTS MALTING PLANT
1913. MANGO PAPPAD (AAM PAPPAD)
1914. MANGO POWDER RIPE
1915. MANGO POWDER
1916. MANGO PROCESSING & CANNING (MANGO PULP)
1917. MEAT PROCESSING (CHICKEN MUTTON)
1918. MEAT PROCESSING (BUFFALO)
1919. MENTHOL BOLD FROM MENTHOL FLAKES
1020. MILK POWDER
1921. MILK POWDER & GHEE
1922. MILK POWDER, GHEE & SPICES
1923. MILK PRESERVATION & MARKETING TO WHOLE SELLERS
1924. MILK PRESERVATION & MARKETING TO WHOLE SELLERS (IN POUCHES)
1925. MILK TOFFEE MANUFACTURES
1926. MINERAL WATER
1927. MINERAL WATER IN POUCHES
1928. MINI FLOUR MILL ATTA MAIDA, SUJI & WHEAT BRAN
1929. MITHAI/HALWAI (SWEET & NAMKEEN)
1930. MUTTON PROCESSING
1931. PAN MASALA (MEETHA, SADA, ZARDA) MAKING & PACKING
1932. PAN MASALA AND POUCH MAKING
1933. PANEER (CHEESE)
1934. PAPAD & BARIYAN
1935. PAPAD PLANT
1936. PEPSICOLA IN POLYTUBES
1937. PETHA PACKAGING
1938. PICKLES
1939. PIGGERY/MEAT/CHICKEN PROCESSING
1940. PINE APPLE JUICE CANNING
1941. POTATO & ONION POWDER
1942. POTATO & ONION FLAKES
1943. POTATO CHIPS
1944. POTATO GRANULES
1945. POUCH FILLING FOR SAUNF SUPARI ILAICHI ETC.
1946. PRESERVATION OF RAWS MANGO JUICE
1947. PROCESSED CHEESE & MARINE PDTS.
1948. PULP FROM TARMARIND
1949. READYMATE PROCESSED FOOD
1950. RICE & CORN FLAKES
1951. RICE BASMATI (TRADING)
1952. RICE POLISHING & PACKAGING IN POUCH
1953. ROASTED/SALTED/MASALA/ CASHEW NUTS ALMONDS & PEA NUT
1954. ROLLER FLOUR MILL

INFOTECH/IT PROJECTS

1955. MEDICAL TRANSCRIPTION
1956. E-COMMERCE
1957. CYBERCAFE
1958. INTERNET SERVICE PROVIDER (ISP)
1959. COMPUTER EDUCATION CENTRE
1960. PORTAL (WEBSITE DESIGN)
1961. CALL CENTRE

TERMS AND CONDITIONS

FOR INDIA

1. Please ask for Quotations of Each *Market Survey Cum Detailed Techno Economic Feasibility Report.* Payable in advance through Draft/M.O./Cash in favour of 'ENGINEERS INDIA RESEARCH INSTITUTE', Delhi. Delivery by Regd.post within 2 Days. (Postage Free)

2. Ask for the Hi-Tech Projects Monthly magazine. Each Magazine covers many Project Profiles for selection of Industry.

FOR OVERSEAS

1. Please ask for Quotations in US $ of Each *Market Survey Cum Detailed Techno Economic Feasibility Report.* Payable in advance through Draft/M.O./Cash in favour of 'ENGINEERS INDIA RESEARCH INSTITUTE', Delhi. (Payable in India) Delivery by Regd.post within 4 Days.

2. Ask for the Hi-Tech Projects Monthly magazine. Each Magazine covers many Project Profiles for selection of Industry.

ENGINEERS INDIA RESEARCH INSTITUTE

4449, Nai Sarak (D), Main Road, Delhi - 110 006 (India)
Ph:. 91-11-23918117, 23916431, 23840361, 31082370
Fax: 91-11-23916431 E-Mail : eirisidi@bol.net.in
Website:www.startindustry.com
Also at : 4/27, Roop Nagar, Near Roop Nagar No. 1 School, Delhi - 110 007 (India) Ph:. 23840361